To the Moon
and Back...To Me

What I Learned from Four Running Feet

Christine Hassing

To PJ,
For your part in teaching me to *hear* and *see*

Dear Reader,

When I had the opportunity to visit the island of Crete, I met a gentleman who shared what would become the foundation to my belief about life. No moment is coincidence. No person crosses our path unplanned. With his finger pointing to the sky, this gentleman spoke, "From somewhere up there you were meant to be here today."

If you are reading *To the Moon and Back...To Me, What I Learned from Four Running Feet*, then I was given the honor of writing what you were meant to *hear*.

There are certain things that are Universal no matter the language, the culture, or where you live. Loss and the grieving process share a commonality: in pain and in promise. Loss doesn't have to be death in the sense of a loved one—two legged or four. Loss is being separated from the safe haven you knew. Marriage, friendship, a job, your home: whatever you loved, needed, or associated with as part of your identity is now absent from your life.

And it's now giving you the opportunity to *transform*.

Yes, this is a story about a dog, and it is more. It is a *journey*—an up-and-down movement through life, like the mantras I recite when I run, repeated until they sink in to the rhythm of each step—a *journey* through the grieving process. And it is a reminder when a loved one leaves Earth, it is never good-bye. It is a story of purpose, of why my path intersected with Roo; if I had not known Roo, I never would have found me. And it is a message about the gift of life and how even in the most painful of times, it is the most beautiful. Instead of wondering why we encountered a painful episode, we can make the fact that it happened matter. It is a story about the ability to *heal*.

A soul fulfilling its purpose inhabits a body that can be covered in fur or in human form. Grieving and finding trust in life and in ourselves is a path we all travel. It knows no discrimination if the one we love—and let go—is a four- or two-legged being, if we are grieving the loss of a job or a home that felt secure, or if we are grieving the loss of who we have been.

Life brings moments we wish wouldn't, or never had to, take place. When we find purpose in each one, we find faith. We find the ability to bravely and gracefully move through life, through every up and down we are certain to experience.

And if we embrace the purpose, we know *unconditional love*.

We often wait for a miracle or an extraordinary event, not realizing that we are being given more than the ordinary in the simplicity of each day. A person facing loss starts to see beauty where their eyes and their heart were clouded by a to-do list or by a sense tomorrow is always guaranteed. When their perspective shifts, what begins to matter most is what someone else still takes for granted. To watch a sunset—to *really* watch a sunset—is nothing short of beautiful and extraordinary.

If we choose to *see*.

From the guidance of a love of my life, I was meant to write this book as you were meant to read at least this opening. If only one sentence in this book touches your heart, the purpose of *To the Moon and Back...To Me: What I Learned from Four Running Feet* will have been achieved.

From Roo and me, we wish you *hope, joy,* and *peace,*
—Christine

Prologue

September 12, 2014

You entered my dream, before you entered this world, then entered my physical life. The child I thought I'd bring into this world became you in my mind. You entered with four legs and a human definition of DOG; you were the soul as my girl, with angel wings from GOD. In my dream, I handed you to your daddy, our family of three, you as our baby girl, to make us better people, to make us complete.

The first night you entered home, you slept as if I were your dog bed, stretched across my chest. My heartbeat a soothing rhythm, the way to lull you to rest. In this room you learned home and learned who was whispering, "I am Mom, always you have my love." In this same room you would whisper, "Mom, always you have my love…I have had enough."

You joined my life just before I came to a fork in the road; would I take the path of least resistance, or would I choose the path of growth? You, with a spirit that saw no boundaries, nudged my fearful spirit to be brave, and your steadfast unconditional love an anchor when I exhibited wavering faith.

You were my coach as I learned to run, knowing I could and would even when I thought, "I am not so sure I can." Your excitement taught me unmeasurable joy in being "right where I am at." Running, our physical activity to parallel learning in life; you my girl, always my teacher alongside.

As I jogged, sprinted, and some moments ran on this path of growth to find the essence of me, you were my sight when I lost my way and my tug when I needed leading. Through my depression, you never let go—you knew I would reach the other side; my wise beautiful girl, believing for both of us when my way I couldn't find. You taught me to increase my ability to *hear* and *see*, to tune into Nature for the messages that can be received. If, on a particular run, you decided we should slow our speed, it was at the most appropriate time when I needed to be reminded that it was not the destination but the journey. If we suddenly increased our speed or immediately started to run, it was when I needed to be reminded "keep going," "you can," "don't fear," or "you are almost done."

You continued to watch me grow toward the center of who I am meant to be. You saw my heart unfolding. You saw me gaining belief in me. You continued to pull me forward and continued to set the pace. "Time out" or "faster," you knew the steps to take. Though neither of us enjoyed the times I had to be out of town, you knew I would come back after what I needed for my growth was found.

As our hearts beat in rhythm to our feet running the trails, you would hear my heart's dreams, your assurance I would not fail. You, the encourager to continue what I was coming to know: that in all things good, and in all things sad, there is always faith and hope. I didn't know consciously (my subconscious hadn't yet found its voice) that you were agreeing to help me with two more lessons of the most ultimate kind—my ownership to keep eyes, ears, and heart open; then the gifts I would find.

Shortly before our runs were to become walks, you and I met a friend; Hawk crossed our path needing our help to lend. We gave him water, we stroked his feathers, we told him he was loved. We looked into his eyes and moved away from ourselves to selflessly honor his spirit, which desired to soar above. He crossed our path as guardian and as a premonition we did not yet see. His message and lesson: the power of setting something free.

He wasn't our first messenger that would give us signs, nor would he be our last. Another of your gifts you gave, teaching me to watch and listen, always messages to guide our path. You whispered, "Let me go," and a grasshopper, a turtle, a robin, a blue heron all served as your aids to help me trust what I heard you say. Moment by moment you gently helped me grow in my trust and faith.

Your ultimate gifts: incredible trust and amazing selfless love; now, as done with Hawk, I must release a piece of my heart to soar and rise above. My dear girl, you knew that I needed to experience firsthand how to see beauty through pain. Oh, what sights and sounds you hear when walking with another on Earth their final days. I am honored and humbled in what I have experienced with you, not just in these final days but in all of our years, my Roo.

I always told you "To the moon and back my love for you" and "You are my right arm." An extension of me, certain irreparable severance if we had to part. I didn't know until you nudged my heart to look it up today—to read the symbolism a few hours before "Go in peace," we would say. "My right arm" is divinely symbolic of *the right hand of God*, and of course, dear Roo, as you and I already know, GOD = DOG.

The last night home, your sleep was you and me together on a bed, my heartbeat willing you to find comfort and rest. In that same room, you learned home, we whispered to each other, "Always, you and me" and "It will be okay—thank you for this journey filled with such beauty." We held you as you prepared to *soar high*, the most precious treasure I will ever touch in my life. My hand over your heart as you set your wings and took flight. One last beat imprinted in the palm of my hand, my right.

And, my beautiful girl, we reinforce all that you strived to teach: that we will see you if we keep open our hearts to find what we seek. Your daddy and I on our walk up the drive tonight; each step is heavy with the weight of not physically seeing you. Trying, so trying, to catch our breaths as grief coursed through. And then the circling right beside us and just above. You sent guardian Hawk whispering, "Mom and Dad, I am well, thank you for your love."

I know it isn't good-bye. I know with us you will always be, and thank you for the other message tonight that you gave me to read. When we feel our chests ache, it is you wagging your tail—the thump a promise always beside us without fail. It read how a dog never dies but sleeps in the warmth of our hearts. So when we can't catch our breath, it is because you, now awake, are whopping your tail very *very* hard.

You entered my dream before you entered this world and before you entered my life. The child I didn't bring into the world in you I would find. Thank you, my beautiful girl, for all you gave your daddy and me; we know love in a way that wouldn't have been possible without you who made us complete. I could not have gotten to the center of me without your guardian love, my Earth angel, now my most precious angel from above.

FAITH

An evening some year before 2005

It is night or day without light. Black and indigo blue, no vibrant colors mixed with these darkest hues. Walking slowly, ever slow; where I might be I do not know. Trees, some standing, some in a lean, some in stagnant water, no longer able to grow leaves. The bark water soaked, ready to fall away. No ripples in the water as dark as the view I face.

I am searching to find…certainly there must be some sign of life. I am alone, and for a few moments I do not fear. More watchful, trying to understand, awaiting light's glimmer to appear. It begins to sink in what my eyes see. I begin to run, my legs gaining speed.

My lungs feel the burn, I am struggling to breathe. But it may catch up; it may grab me away from this racing to leave. I am scared, I am terrified. Where is there safety I can find? Up ahead, a building, perhaps someone will rescue me. Closer, as if it is the finish line, "Help me make it," my tearful plea. Silence still, but a wall to embrace my back; against it, sliding to the ground, I collapse.

The kind of sobbing that shudders the body pours from the depths of my soul. I cannot shake the panic that has taken control. *No moon, nor sunlight, no sign of any life. Into the eyes of the dying I stared, death striving to catch me in its snare.*

As breath leaves, my chest is held in a tighter squeeze. "But I do not want this," I call out from somewhere deep. No one to respond; silence greets the words I cry. Or maybe they weren't said aloud, my voice skilled at staying buried inside. I must run, I must run far away. Right where I am, I cannot stay.

I blink, I gasp for air. My location, I am uncertain where. A wall to my right, to my left, someone lies next to my side. "Where am I now?" I try to focus my eyes. My bedroom, my husband, familiar surroundings. The relief it was not reality but just a dream. Or was it a warning if I did not heed?

My soul dying, my heart starting to decay. My life on a course to darkness. And I begin to run, searching for change.

September 20, 2014

"Don't micromanage the soul," was once said to me. Words meant to encourage the stopping of analyses. So much easier to slice, dice, turn, and find the explanation why—*head space* versus *heart space* is going on inside.

I reflect on moments that take place as we walk our life path, those times that are the memories that linger and last. Those memories we refer back to, that stand out, that time does not erase. Perhaps those are the moments we shift from head space. In those moments etched, a cast, a mold that does not fade. I believe those are the moments our hearts are opening, our souls awake.

Some memories, imprinted never to leave, come back as a knock to revisit, heal, then move forward with ease. Other memories we make a choice to immediately embrace, allowing readiness for the new, for a change. We may not be aware of how powerful this accumulation of memories will become and how each will define the world we *see*. Nor how certain memories will become more significant in their meaning. But the soul knows the gift of each memory we tuck away, and it awaits the courage our heart will find to grow in love, hope, and faith.

A memory etched, a treasured moment I hold; no words to explain, no micromanagement of the soul. Our souls, with the gift of our bodies to carry our hearts, we ran, our feet in harmony to the morning start. There, in the trees, the most beautiful eyes watched us, talked with us, then graced above us both with its glorious wings; the majestic owl in flight over us, a magical time shared together, us three. Together, in our final walk of your life, often that memory came to mind.

Today, the bike ride extended to paths we shared as we ran. I ask you to send either Hawk or Owl so that I know we are still on the trail hand-in-hand. At first, it was the wings gliding to the tree and when I asked it to pose for a picture, those beautiful eyes again looked at me. The owl, in the same spot where the three of us met, as my angel whispered, "I did as you asked." Always to the moon and back, never apart. For Earth and Heaven do not separate what is joined as one in our hearts.

I reflect on moments that take place as we walk our life path, those times that are the memories that linger and last. Those memories we refer back to, that stand out, that time does not erase—today, a moment when feeling my heart far greater than any head space. In this moment etched, a cast, a mold that will never fade; my heart so bare yet still open, my soul gaining strength not to break. Perhaps it is in those shifting moments our souls further unite; and we grow into oneness from darkness to radiant light.

September 25, 2014

I close my eyes and see each stepping stone behind me, the path I have walked woven in harmony. One, two, a billion four hundred fifty million and a few more, each needing the other, each with a purpose it was put there for.

I love to see how the pieces fit together, the whys, the "ah, of course," the knowing nods as I reminisce. As clarity whispers in the rewind, "Look at all of the gifts." So divinely orchestrated, look how a moment that happened set the stage for another moment to take place. Act one…Act four, complete stories made.

With my eyes still closed, now turned to the path ahead, I think of where I stand in *now*, gratitude for where I've been. I reflect on moments I know will come and see the threads bound to what occurred *then*, preparing for a new experience with you, my beautiful girl, one of my "bestest" friends.

The seventh race of this year approaches; my excitement for it has grown since signing up. Not *seeing* then what this race would come to mean, what would change for us. Our angels knew what was best when they nudged me, "This is the one"— one of those moments that set the stage for what was to come.

You have been my inspiration, my coach, my fan; you have taken every step with me reminding me "I can." Saturday, we will run again, you the wind in my legs and in my soul. And with each mile to twenty-six, together we will reach the goal.

I find it true to your courageous and bold spirit that you asked the angels to have me run this particular day—the day you moved from my dream to the world, on your ninth birthday. I know our souls agreed we would take this part of the road together, you, Earth angel at my side; still, there are many *many* moments I wish I had bargained for more time.

But just as angels nudged me to this race, you nudged me with a reminder this week. I am supposed to be the person my dog knows me to be. I am supposed to look forward in trust to the stepping stones that await. I am supposed to walk forward in *knowing* faith. We know our souls connected heart-to-heart; you may not physically be seen, but you are not far.

With my eyes still closed, now turned to the path ahead, I think of where I stand in *now*, gratitude for where I've been. I reflect on moments I know will come and see the threads bound, intertwined, you and me; I will continue to watch and hear—and feel—how you are always with me.

September 28, 2014

A parallel to life, we often realized on our runs; so often we found symbolism during or after we were done. "It is the journey not the destination"—it's true what they say. Take time to pause, goals need room for flexibility, make sure to play. Joy in surprises, focusing on *now* helps you go farther than you can see. Mountains are not roadblocks, make sure in the rain you sing.

Yesterday, as the marathon began, there they were again to whisper their melody of comfort and longevity, the sandhill cranes flying over me. They had been my sky guides on the morning runs, when you were still resting before our days had begun. They knew the rhythm of my steps were speaking, "I wish you and I were on the trail, instead of only me," and their angelic tone would soothe me into a place of peace. Their lyrics said longevity, assurance in their tone, "always" was their chorus as I made my way to you at home. Yesterday, their song was whispering, "You can go the distance, you are not alone. Longevity, always love, to you from up above."

My heart is in gratitude for how you rally the Universe to respond when I need a boost in faith, ensuring communication in a variety of ways. Your daddy there at mile nine, thirteen, and seventeen; a smile, a hug, wishes to have fun, unending encouragement for me. Or when I had one of those "not quite enough" moments, you sent a kind soul, his assurance—there were many other runners behind me still miles to go. And when I wasn't doubting I could, but needed an extra boost, there on my path an angel's stamp: "You are loved. We believe in you."

Today, the day after, I falter, missing your physical form. Missing those eyes telling me, "I don't care that you raced, it is time for more." You whisper, "Mom, remember, we had yesterday; a bike ride today will be okay." As I start down the trail, first the additional angel stamps—two feathers placed on my path. And then the beautiful gift, like the arms of a hug, Hawk circling in a half moon, our added symbol of unconditional love.

As I thought about the race, and it's parallel to life, how it took me to an edge of faith was brought to mind. It tested my will, it relied on my trust no matter how uphill. It required *leaning in* to the full experience, knowing there would be so many gifts *on the other side*: gifts not seen but felt, which are the best kind. It required bringing focus into *now* and only *right here* and, baby girl, I thank you for every whisper when you reminded me to focus on "the journey, don't worry beyond what is near." It required me to see the beauty that surrounded every step I made, not just externally, but within, through the transformation undoubtedly taking place. And as my heart expanded into and through the experience of the race, oh, what incredible love being learned and taking place.

A parallel to life, we often realized on our runs; so often we found symbolism during, or in reflecting, once we were done.

Yesterday, you, as my guardian angel, and I, in honor of you, ran in that race, the symbolism a mirror to our time together in your last days. The most beautiful time during the hardest leaning in; by not stopping, by trusting, amazing gifts I win.

Not the victor medal, nor the shirt tangible as they are, but the realization that when you think you can't take another step, you can go beyond, no matter how hard.

September 30, 2014

Always such laughter, such amusement in my soul; how I loved our zig and zag to sidestep as if walking on snow. You were not a fan of those clusters of leaves, intermittent like throw rugs in our way; I would giggle and ask, "What will we do when no bare dirt remains where our footsteps are placed?" I loved our dance with the leaves as fall grew more vibrant, more bold. I, the follower to you, the lead as the season started to unfold.

This morning, you whispered, "Flexibility" and "Openness to change." I wanted to sidestep, and you wanted me to stand in place.

We still aren't able to eat breakfast at home—no favorite signal of yours that it is time for toast. This morning, it feels like a double loss—not just the one loss that is now our reality. Adorned in bravery for the sake of what I believe your daddy needs, keep my tears in check as his pour down his cheeks. Memories that bring a smile are yet hard to view too; memories that when relived are now a reminder of meals not the same without you.

The joy of you "just knowing" when the timer was about to ring, and oh, your tap of the foot reminding your daddy to share whatever we had to eat. The void not allowing our hearts to repair, both of us not able to speak of the fear in the air. Love had grown deeper in our home of three; could two keep it feeling complete? Would I pull inward and shut Daddy out of my pain (a long-standing capability I have been trying to untrain)? Or would I help Daddy feel needed as we both grieved, so that our grieving would not be done independently? Your daddy has felt my dependence grow, my comfort in embracing the surefootedness of home. Now that home has teetered off base, will my urge return to not run to, but to run away?

The sadness deepening in my heart, and then your whisper, "Change your sight and look for new starts." With the Universe your team, messages hop across the road. Rabbits symbolize the power of my thoughts—positive thoughts beget positive, negative should be let go. With that reminder, on through the day I went; striving to focus on the gift of timing in the messages sent.

With the warm weather, the beautiful fall night beckoning me, in the Jeep to one of our trails for a walk, I envision you in your front seat. Slow, ever so slow, as I asked my ego to step aside so my heart could hear and see, I started to see those throw rugs tossed along the path, and a smile was forming within me. I asked you to show me a sign that you were walking with me, immediately following was the angel stamp in gray, a feather whispering, "Peace."

On the way back from the turn around, with the wind you reminded me, how in the soft breeze we felt as though kissed from angel wings. Often it was that boost of encouragement needed at the time. Onward our rhythm, your feet with mine. Tonight the wind picked up, the leaves fell from the trees, and suddenly I felt an urge to twirl with my arms in the air feeling a joyful glee.

I started trying to capture a picture of the floating leaves, and you, who always listens, tried again to please. I would ask for another swirl of wind to try to capture a snapshot, and you would guide the Universe to respond. But not fast enough with the button before leaves fell beyond. Looking up, I would try again and again, and once more you would drop a leaf, and then I realized laughing returned, like our dance of zig and zag, you and me.

Always such laughter, such amusement in my soul; how I loved our zig and our zag to sidestep as if snow. You were not a fan, but I think you sidestepped just to hear me giggle and feel how in love I was (and am) with you; you have always been about giving, my beautiful baby girl Roo.

A picture texted to your daddy who awaits my return home, the path leading me to where I am meant to go.

I am learning to run away

Beside me outdoors, next to me in my room, is the only one I'm most comfortable talking out loud to. We walk past the garage; we walk the half-circle driveway past the aisle of trees. Ever a listening ear, always acceptance of me. Others can't see the friend always by my side. Companionship for me, yet imaginary in my mind.

I sit on a stool watching what he makes. A piece of wood added with another as something takes shape. I love the many jars of screws he sometimes reaches to use. Organized in drawers or on a wall, his array of tools. I am in a boat learning to cast a line, the peaceful water reflecting his patience by my side. I am in a loft of the camper as he and Grandma turn off the lights, a smile and a softly said "goodnight." I am a center of their attention, without having to talk frequently; I can be quiet, the three of us content together without the need to speak. I can be with them and not have to be home; where I live I feel unsure...and alone.

October 3, 2014

I am reminded of the robin in the morning as you and I lay awake. At first I thought it was her dance of joy or she was shaking off the rain. Through the picture window, from the inside out, I watched, and watched more. She, unconditionally loving her children, her comfort through the storm. I, indoors, where it was dry, yet I too was doing the same. Unconditionally in love with you, focused on the gifts we shared in this "storm" we faced.

I am not sure the exact time the shift started to occur; when *from* started to stop and *toward* I turned. Perhaps it was this year as snow began to melt and spring was peeking through. Or maybe it was when I opened the e-mail nine years ago to look at six brothers and sisters, and your face my soul knew. Home would come to define what complete meant, the enjoyment of "hanging out" as our family unit. Each weekend that the three of us could "hold down the sofa" as your daddy would say, always the perfect start to contented days.

I was told once that like the bee and honey so sweet, life would feel amazingly easy if I discovered how to just *be*. The "sweet spot" of peace would be when I could stand still, allow, trust what I could not see; for when I learned to be quiet, the most spectacular view would be clear in front of me.

It wasn't just the last miles of our run on Earth where I learned the blessings of *now* and the power of faith. I had been learning how to *see* and *hear* what was whispered in messages every moment of each day. But, oh my baby girl, what an immense treasure you gave; the depth of trust and love I learned *letting go* of the reins.

Sitting in the yard with you, relishing the feelings; observing the art of Nature, listening to its melodies; the birds calling each other and soaring up high and the wind playing in the trees; a chirping cricket, the orange hue forming in the leaves. There was no place to be except in the *now* of this time with you. In the stillness, so much clarity coming through.

You helped me increase my ability to see, hear, and feel, and you helped me find the "sweet reward" of standing still. In our last miles, you promised beside me you would always be— if I had the courage to *let go* in a leap of faith and *believe*. Now I watch, I listen, I keep my heart open, and I quietly take each step. And true to your word, you show me how you have never left. Perhaps you send an owl, a hawk, a lyric to a song, or you find a way to enter my dream; in whatever way you whisper at my side, you are with me.

As I hear the rain drumming a song in concert against the roof above, I am reminded of the robin, a mother's unending love. Through the picture window, from the inside out, I watched, and watched more as she unconditionally loved her children, her comfort through the storm. She, too, would face letting her children go, to let them soar to new heights, her focus on giving them food to prepare them for flight. Her love so grand, she would enable them to go, taking with them her trust and immense unconditional love.

The robin and I, our only difference is our place in the rain, our love for another very much the same.

October 5, 2014

It was just a floor, a floor that can be made clean again; dirt no comparison to our blessings in the form of friends. But two scrubbings and still the spill seen; my discouragement, I knew, was something deeper in me. I had yet to understand what it might mean.

Out for breakfast (I know you watch how Daddy and I haven't found our seats at the kitchen counter yet). Upon returning home, we removed the balloon from the mailbox, one of the last party remnants. I felt the urge to let it go—I know, sending it into the sky is not new. I now have an appreciation for others who find comfort in the gesture as they watch the rising balloon.

Then to the trail, the urge to go for a run, reminiscent of our routine on a weekend before a warm sun. As I drove to one of our starting points, taking our Jeep, the urge so strong to reach across to you in your front seat. But just like other moments that remind me you are there yet it has changed, the reality of your physical absence jolts my heart's rhythmic state.

Mantras to match the rhythm of each step forward repeated through my mind, ones of gratitude turned to a request for help that I might find. "It was just a floor. A floor that can be made clean. Help me understand what is weighing on me." Each step reaching deeper, the answer rising, closer, and closer yet, and there it was right at the edge.

Like a bottle that shatters, that cracks open, that spills forth in a gush, so too from my heart *it* was about to rush. It was going to crack open my resolve, it was going to test my faith; if I allowed it to bubble to the top, it too would spill, all over it would splay. A clean floor symbolized "neat and tidy," kept in order, in control, like emotions that we want to remain positive, not wanting the ones that acknowledge we feel a hole. It was sorrow, it was the tenderness not yet healed; it was pain, reminding just how much sorrow is real.

Today, I miss you, baby girl, well, that is nothing new, but heartache today is flowing through. I let the tears stream, and I keep going as you taught, trying to bring focus to the beautiful colors of fall. Your whisper in the sun peeking through the trees, "Mom, I am here, always you and me." I drive home with a heaviness not so strong, but still it rides along my side; and then, again, your love sent a sign in the sky.

Across my path, so eloquently, so majestically, your whisper, "Always at your side," more tears, this time of joy, of awe, of love, as Hawk soared by. Thank you, my dear Roo, for your message always with me, your reminder to believe.

The words from the movie replaying in an edited language I can embrace—your gentle reminder to feel and not just say. "I have spent so long trying to keep the book safe, I started to forget to practice its message of faith."

It was just a floor. A floor that can be made clean again; and I am in gratitude for the accidental spill by a friend. If the bottle had not broken, had not interjected into my safety net of *control*, I would not have found the grace in affirmation of what is so precious to hold. Trust, faith, hope, three promises that always remain true. I may not see you, my beautiful girl, but you I will never lose. Beside me you are in the front seat of the Jeep and next to me as we run, curled up at my feet with the day's setting sun. To the moon and back, never good-bye, always you and me. "Keep your eyes, ears, and heart open, see...there is me!"

October 8, 2014

The last two mornings as I look into the sky, reflecting back at me a clear starry light. My mind steps back, where my heart still resides, to our early mornings, our late nights. My feet matching yours, bare in the dew-filled grass, as we scouted, I learned from you how to quiet time's tendency to rush past.

Someone said to me once that when you encounter another, you are fulfilling a Divine appointment, a purpose to why you should meet; I like to take that thought further—a puzzle finding completion with one more piece. This thought has occurred to me as I reflect on these past two days, what imprints we leave along the way. When two people's connection begins to unite as one whole, perhaps in that merging we stamp our surroundings with slivers of our souls.

When we are drawn to where we've been, when whispers call us back to where our footprints are still seen, it is then that our souls reaffirm what we know; we reclaim what we believe. Yesterday, on our trail, you orchestrated a symphony for me, a rhythm for each step with my feet. Birds in song, chipmunks that you and I would periodically join in a playful dance, the deer, the squirrels, all friends present, often we would run to, with, or past.

You whispered, "Mom, remember how I taught you to listen, to hear? How in Nature's words we stood near? Now breathe and let go. If you are quiet, you will know. Embrace the gifts, embrace the messages, find the joy in Nature we always did; in you, through you, beside you, I always live." I heard what sounded like rain coming behind me fast, but it was just the most splendid wind in the leaves, yet another angel stamp. Then I crossed the intersection and the most vivid chirp caused me to turn my head; a cricket talking, like the one you had taught me to hear when we sat outside on your dog bed.

The rabbit we had slowed down for and ran after fast, hopped across the path for me to see; joy knocking again as I felt you with me. Tonight it was the black squirrel, a glint in his eye of "Yes! You get it now," as he scampered by. And your message, "Right beside you, Mom, at your side." Earlier, I told a dear friend I am okay but miss having that utter and completely uninhibited on-clouds happiness when I felt so complete. In this run, I am moving one step closer to that feeling with the encouragement you still teach.

The last two mornings, as I look into the sky, reflecting back at me a clear starry light. My mind steps back, where my heart still resides, to every early morning, all of our late nights. When two people's connection united as one whole, in our surroundings we leave the imprints of our souls. You led me to where our souls blended as one, and slivers still remain, and you whisper, you affirm, "Hope, love, faith." Your reminders abundant, my heart in gratitude as you help me reclaim what I believe; I may not physically see you as you, but with me you will always be.

October 12, 2014

I wonder the criteria for when a dam unleashes the pent-up water it has held at bay; is it when the walls begin to feel the weight? Or maybe it is an automatic trigger that says, "Now is the day." Is it when it is time for a fresh supply? Time to begin anew? Or perhaps it is to repair cracks where water is seeping through. My heart the dam, my tears the water, the last few days the unleashed, no longer can I contain. And through it all you whisper, "Hope, love, faith."

It began with the struggle of feeling vulnerable and the gift received; to talk with one who so unconditionally accepts me as me. I try to find my footing again, the foundation that once felt complete. Now requiring redefinition, you as angel still, yet differently for your daddy and me. I described it to someone: on so many levels I am at peace, but there is also an incredible emptiness felt deep. As my sister gave me her time, her ears, her heart, and her *knowing* without having to describe, she gave me the gift of joy as tears began to slide. The tears were from laughter, one of those moments when laughter bursts from souls, and I could hear you whisper, "It is okay to be happy; let the sadness go."

A second weekend away since our guardian above you became. Will I ever stop pausing when I reach for the luggage, thinking I should wait so you don't see? (We sure struggled, didn't we, baby girl, each time I was about to leave.) Your daddy and I North this weekend to four-wheel with the Jeep. I am trying to keep joy in place, but at times, knocking at my heart stronger is grief.

Your greeting, "You're home!" missing when we entered the door brought a longing in my ego way. Walking the tightrope of knowing you are still with us, yet not physically seeing you, poked at my soul's faith. Yet again, you arranged with the Universe what I would need when I greeted this day—today an anniversary—four weeks ago, thirty days past, when you whispered, "It is time, it is okay." There majestically in the tree, watching the yard as you always had too, my beautiful Hawk, your messenger to say, "Always together, Mom, me and you."

Throughout the day you kept me reminded of hope, faith, and love; so many signs sent, so many gifts from above. The feather on my path, an angel's note written to say, "Blessed, thankful, our lives, this day." The deer with her message of "gentleness, love, and peace"; a drive to the trail the first time on the route with you "virtual" in the front seat. And on the run, after I paused to leave tears where we often stood, you reminded me the parallels of running and life, and how I could...and would. Each step of my feet bringing clarity to where we go from here, not the destination but the journey; *lean in*, trust, let go of any fear.

More tears tonight, reminding me that in pain is splendid beauty; with an open heart so many gifts we receive. A wonderful conversation with your daddy—he is always *in tune* to what my soul needs to hear. The right words at the right times, hope and trust again brought near. When he isn't busy handing me the world…oh wait, he did again just by giving his unconditional love; he too, another of my Earth angels sent from above. And as if you, my dear Roo, wanted to make sure I was steadfast in what my heart was reaffirming it believed, there on the branch, in awe I viewed Hawk again in his splendor, his guardian message *see*.

I wonder the criteria for when a dam unleashes its pent-up water it has held at bay. Is it because it has broken, no longer able to hold up faith? Is it when it desires to let in the *new* so that it doesn't risk stopping air flow if it were to no longer move? Or, perhaps, it is timing waiting for signs, signals, and cues. Maybe it knows something much bigger and controls when it is time to let go. And when it is time to have faith in what will be, perhaps it just allows the ebb and flow.

Maybe it's a fortress, already certain all things happen as they are meant to take place, recognizing there is peace in allowing each moment to happen as it may. My heart the dam, my tears the water, the last few days a willingness to no longer contain. Through it all, affirmation "Hope, love, faith."

October 15, 2014

You have gently led me back to our time in those days as life was bringing into view significant change. In the stars this morning, in the play of the squirrels darting across the drive; in the thankful walk of the turkeys, in the melody of the cranes flying by—with each your whisper, "Remember the faith you gained." An easing up on the part of grief today.

As my mind rewinds, my heart pulls back to the beauty and the awe. I am reminded of when I let go of the reins, when I no longer feared "What if I fall?" I am back in those moments when peace knocked and I opened the door and learned a whole new level of love never known before. I am in that *now* walking alongside, listening, hearing in ways brand new, my soul having such amazing conversations with you.

I momentarily drift to the days before I loosened my grip, moments when I could feel my footing slip. I am on the trail alone because the distance is too great for you, my mind screaming, "Run far away," but my legs unable to move. I am clinging to signs, like a leaf-shaped heart at my next step, my soul quiet as my mind says, "See, I knew it, not yet." I am in the shower unable to tell which stream of water is faster, stronger, more cleansing. For in each tear that falls, there is a greater listening. As you softly bring me back to your dying days, I can feel again the shift from fear to trust I made.

You told me what you wanted, you told me what you expected of me. You assured me that though your appearance would change, still my angel you would always be. You expect me to be messenger of beauty in pain and the power of love, hope, and faith. You expect me to make it count, this gift you agreed to give. And you wanted to know you were contributing to inspiration; how through me you would still live. You expect me to take your teaching of the power of leaning in, to not run from, but immerse wholly into the moments at hand, to ask grace and gratitude to be the lead in sadness's dance.

You have nudged me, like your eagerness did when it was time for our canoe, Jeep, or a run. Your reminder "Mom, you must, don't lose sight of the depth of your *knowing*, of how I taught you trust." Like so many times before, you are pulling me to the next mile mark as you remind me *can*, and you are pulling me back on the trail to remind me *purpose* and *plan*.

You are bringing chipmunks, soft breezes, and the gentle message from the deer to remind me to stay quiet, stand still, and *hear*. You heard my dreams, to be a "change the world needs," and you are whispering "all things connect; help others *see*." Every single second holds a reason why it takes place, and there is more than what meets the eye, so stand firmly on trust, unwavering faith. All dots that seem fragmented do come together at the appropriate time—a "no" brings opportunity to know "yes"; opposites teach us best, I find.

Today, the mirror reflected eyes with a look I haven't seen; there was a tiny glint, a spark of light, a little speck—is that hope trying to wink at me?

You have gently led me back to when we were together in those days when life brought into view such significant change. Like the ones you and I both wished upon when looking at the stars; in the play of the squirrels that tell me—right next to me you are. In the elegant flight of the three cranes that have been a symbol of Daddy, you, and me, you reminded me to stand strong in what I believe. Hope, faith, love, complete and unconditional, the immense power of trusting when we can't see; be in the now, don't rush ahead, pause, quiet, breathe.

October 19, 2014

My soul visualizes I am in a boat floating across open water, soft, almost no waves as far as I can see; the horizon behind and in front are not visible to me. I close my eyes and raise my face to the sun; I am at peace, with trust, I am one. Then I reach the finish line, the end of a race; and there, as the waves grow stronger and higher, I am riding out a storm's rising rage.

I hold on to the sides, certain the turbulence will ease; rapidly I repeat, "Believe, believe, I believe." And then, there you are, whispering, "I am with you," and my racing heart slows; I feel the boat's rocking stop, no longer its ferocious to and fro. But you know my soul is transforming, that my heart needs time to heal, and the best way to do that is to move through—not around—what I feel. I am in shallow water, you don't want me to have to tread deep; and suddenly a wave capsizes me, tears flow down my cheeks.

I am upright soon, floating across still waters again, the sun's glow reminding me "I can, I will." My eyes closed, I am back to our trail, and again, I feel stilled. Once more, I feel the calm water start to stir and wake. But you whisper, "Let's go. It's okay. We are about to enjoy a favorite way to start our weekend day." You reminded me that you taught me to listen to all that surrounds me, to "drink in" what I see; and immersed, I became in the birds' songs, the crunch of the leaves, the yellows weaved among the greens.

I am now physically sitting in my sister's living room, partnering with Mom to complete finishing touches for the upcoming wedding day; I am at peace, as one with faith. I feel the warmth and love of my sister's home, and I am content, filled with joy, feeling cradled in unconditional love. I feel safe, full of hope; I am excited at what the future holds. Ahead, I can *see* Mom, my sister, and her baby makes three, all of them securely surrounding me.

"Home is where the heart is," you whispered on our trail today; it doesn't have to be your own four walls, it doesn't have to be just one place. It is where you feel love, where the giving and receiving are exchanged; it is wherever souls have connected, it is where the heart feels safe. It is where footprints have been etched, a permanence to revisit and meet each other again and again; it is where future memories will be made and where new chapters begin. It is when I am at my sister's, or Mom's, time shared anywhere with them, with your daddy, or with others dear to me. It is when I am in the Jeep next to your front seat or on our trail or in the comfort of your whispers, "With you, always, the moon, you and me."

My soul visualizes I am in a boat floating across open water, soft, almost no waves as far as I can see; the horizon behind and in front are not visible to me. I close my eyes and raise my face to the sun; I am at peace, with trust, I am one.

October 23, 2014

Longevity. Longevity of mums, cut stems, in a vase of water, three weeks and still they radiantly shine. Longevity, the message of the sandhill crane, alone, its flight following our afternoon drive. Longevity of love that distance and time cannot separate, that continually reveals *always*, that transcends space.

Sunday was no exception to the relishing of a lazy start, at least momentarily, before the reality you weren't waiting jump-started my heart. I kept my eyes closed *seeing* you peeking over the back of the couch, ready for me to join you and Daddy already starting the lazy lounge. You would watch for me to get my spot, then my leg warmer you would quickly be, and there I became snuggled between my two loves, our family. I kept my eyes closed and sent to you and the Universe a wish: may the day ease how strongly your physical presence I miss.

Behind closed eyes, I could *see* in my mind the trees, two sections of tops separate, forming a "V." And then, it came into the open space, hovering with its fast beating wings; a vision of a hummingbird urging joy, the symbol it brings.

As I reflect on each day since then, I have felt longer durations of lightheartedness again. I realize that ever so softly yet steadily and sure, joy has begun to inch in to overcome the sadness, the hurt. Running or a bicycle ride past where we integrated with Owl—such a special day. And sharing written words for others, the gift you've helped me refine in *hearing* what to say. And being a part of assisting my mom to find her finishing touches for her ensemble as mother of the bride. And just like Saturday, resting warmly, my heart is at one of its "homes" as my mom, sis, and I share time.

Driving in the dark, talking with you, and then there you were saying, "Hi Mom, I love you too." The most beautiful outstretched "arms" as you flew across my path, Owl with its wise message and a reminder, always our love will last.

Standing in the dress that I will be wearing when she says "I do," the honor of standing beside my sister as her dream comes true. As I look in the mirror I saw it once again, its reflection smiling, a "knowing" nod and a wink; in its radiance, its assurance, its promise of longevity, there is hope looking back at me.

Longevity. Longevity of mums still shining, their vibrancy disconnected from their base, you joining us on the Ranger ride, as a guide in the sandhill crane. Longevity of love, distance cannot separate. Souls connected, Earth and above, one space.

October 26, 2014

Quietly, peacefully, yet boldly, the day whispers, "Time to awake." Such a spectacular view, my opportunity to partake.

I am reflecting on our run yesterday, the eighth race of the year, and each step I took, how you were near. When I was at mile eleven I felt you leashed with my waist, hearing you say, "Soon will be the finish to the race." I felt you, the wind in my legs and the beat in my heart, reminding me how many times you kept going even when it was hard. I didn't know—at least in the human layers that protect our sight, you were putting up a fight. I didn't know that the avenue you had selected to leave Earth was already coursing through you; I hadn't yet listened that your time to leave would be soon. Protecting me until I was ready, not yet on our runs did you pause or slow for me; more you wanted to teach, unfading imprints you had yet to leave.

With your spirit of strength and unconditional love the fuel in my soul, onward my legs carried me; just one more mile to go. And then, your reminder love holds me close; at mile thirteen dear friends cheering, "Go go go!" One close friend running near the finish line, then another joining my other

34

side. A power of three to lift and affirm I can; the run, as in life, their outstretched hands. Another friend there with a hug and then there he was, your daddy's eyes full of love.

Just to make sure I knew your happiness in what we achieved, there where I stood, you laid a feather for me. I *see* your eyes sparkling, and I feel your wet water kiss; another great time together, our souls in bliss.

Your daddy and I walked the island later that day, and I knew what you had to say. "Mom, just like when you came home after sneaking out the door to go compete, my insistence it was now my turn, your time with me. We would walk a few miles, peace and joy our companions each step made; you would feel you were in Heaven—"Please don't wake me," you would say. Today, as you walk with Daddy, hand-in-hand, hearts entwined; fall colors and sun, peace and promise, with each step you find. Alongside as companion on your path, I can feel your heart flutter resting in assurance our love will last."

With stillness, in a majestically radiant way, the sun whispers, "It is time for a new day." Its light an assurance, an inkling of the new, and its rise affirmation that every twenty-four hours, beginnings do shine through. In each step of our runs, in each footprint forward in life, there you are, always at my side.

October 28, 2014

It sneaks up, it enters without choice to open the door; I would like to say it doesn't even knock, but hindsight reflects it may hint before. It sits down in a corner, at first patiently waiting for a "hello," and if it senses neglect, its urging to take notice grows. It edges closer, it wraps you in a hug, it encourages you to lean on it, encouraging you to let go.

It would have you think it is not friend but foe to peace, until you allow it to fully be with you, this "it" called grief.

I would prefer the joy I find in raking leaves; I lost count of how many sticks under leaves you left for me. You loved to "dance" with them, picking one up in your teeth, then your burst of giddiness to run with such glee. As I raked the leaves along the edge of the drive, I knew you were by my side. That drive holds imprints of many a footstep you and I made, part of the route of our yard laps we would take. I would laugh at how you would be steps ahead of me; and my giggles immense as your eyes sparkled in eagerness at our routine. You would dart down the sidewalk; was the driveway our start this time? And if I turned right, like the sound of a horse catching up, you galloped past my side.

To affirm that you were keeping me company, you left one of your reminder signs: the blanket of leaves I couldn't see under, there for me to find. I had been thinking of what the leaves and grass could represent, the grass to my right, now uncovered where I had been. Ahead, unseen by the browns, oranges, and reds, vibrancy in what is next. The leaves cover the path yet to take, the grass symbolic of what steps we have already made. Sure, knowing there is grass makes it easier to trust stepping forward in faith, but there is still fun surprise underneath that awaits. It could be a stick, it could be a mole hole, or it could be a tiny white feather whispering, "Hello." Just as we may see life's goals and dreams urging us to take steps forward though we can't fully *see*, we have to do so with trust, not fear, with believing in possibility.

The joy continued when I lay down in the grass, just like when we were "yard lizards" watching summer clouds float past. I felt the grass between my fingers, and I listened to Nature as you had taught me to do, and I drank in the *now* letting happiness flow through.

But today "it" visited, it nudged, it said, "It is time to expand and grow. We know your faith, but you need to take it slow." And once again, baby girl, you reminded me one of the mantras as we ran, not the destination but the journey, when we give away fear, we are handed *can*. I was reminded how I love races when I don't know the course ahead and that you always have to go through, not around, because reaching deep within is when you feel best. I struggle to be home, the human in me keeps repeating, "Empty and not the same," and my soul reminds me "allow" and "gifts await on the other side of this pain." To know more trust, it comes when tested in faith; greater joy through knowing *without* so what we have we will abundantly embrace.

It sneaks up, it enters, it sits down in a corner, it edges closer, it wraps you in a hug, encourages you to lean on it, encouraging you to let go. In the tears that serve as rain to help a flower grow, my heart starts to heal as I let sadness flow. Grief is a friend if we choose to partner with it through our trust and hope, that never-gone bond of love I am coming to know. In time, home will become home again in new ways not yet seen, and you will love the changes for always with us you will be.

October 30, 2014

"The kitchen is where the heart is," a dear friend once said to me; today, the words replaying, affirmation of truth indeed.

Grandma by my side as I soften butter, mix, and bake; her encouragement to trust—not exactly measuring, but with a dash and pinch—that was her gifted way. And the love of my spice cupboard, I am not sure if it's simply because I enjoy the chance to create, or maybe it is another family connection to Grandma or Mom or my sister who knows seasonings by smell and taste.

And *seeing* you, my kitchen helper, as I stir, open the oven, or prepare to load the dishwasher—oh the "dance" we would do. So insistent to help prewash, that was you! In the adding of ingredients your waiting eyes, perhaps something will spill, fall, be accidentally dropped by your side. And the oven's timer, music to your ears, and your excitement as it must have meant eating time was near. You: an extension of my leg from oven to counter just in case I needed help setting food down. You made sure the dishwasher need not work too hard, your willingness to clean as a first round.

I heard the whisper a couple of nights ago, a solidity to

what I believe; that when an image so vivid enters our minds, it is our guardian angels next to us we see. You were there to escort me as soon as the timer beeped; I knew you would soon be two steps ahead of me, letting Daddy know it was time to eat.

People who have the opportunity to talk with loved ones who watch them from above will learn the many ways they are not alone, still surrounded by who they love. Perhaps it is when they are sleeping or when they are driving to a specific event, or when they are quietly sitting, or tucking children into bed. Or perhaps when they are decorating a holiday tree or when their tears stopped in the instant they felt a sense of peace. Or in the bloom of a flower or in the flight of Owl or Hawk or a feather at my feet; one of the many ways you let me know you are right next to me.

Just like you strived to be of assistance from oven to counter to plate, I know you are wanting to help us refind home as our base. I know you were there when grief knocked on my heart's door, and you've been finding ways to steer my soul toward knowing in all things there is purpose for. You opened my ears yesterday to all that your daddy said; he has a way of saying things that make me feel hope and promise in the wonderfulness that lies ahead. This morning, you flew through the trees as Hawk, your colors radiantly shining against the leaves. "Good morning, still watching over you, always I will be. Enjoy your breakfast and remember toast for me."

Today, joy was our partner in the kitchen of...home. My heart in contentment, resting warmly in trust, I am not alone. Angels that once held down rugs while on Earth don't stop waiting, watching, helping to guide; they just find new ways to be at our side. "The kitchen is where the heart is"—such truth in this. Thank you for giving me yet another gift. Today in the mixing, stirring, baking, I found the ability to find comfort where I had not been able to stay. The "heart of home," I stand in place.

And I run further to where I can't be seen

I feel special, I feel loved; when that joyful smile and tone offers food, to them it must mean I am "enough." The tradition that each meal ends with dessert offers me the opportunity to receive, having a favorite snack readily available, the message "you matter to me." I don't have to share anything that may be on my mind; I only have to say, "Thank you" with grateful eyes. The more sugary the dessert, fear is fed, comfort fleeting. Salty chips with dip masking insecure feelings. Food an abundance to stifle the lacking; food to reinforce the only certainty I could see. Each spoonful, each fork raised to eat, will keep others from wanting to look at me.

I don't need to be watched, old enough for "on my own" days; but companionship for each other so each day at her home I stay. I am shadow when running errands, I am shadow in the house. I am assistant when the multiple raspberry bushes call out, "Pick us now." Like the comfort of grandparents, where I can "just" be, with her I can also stay hidden from being seen. She has that same prideful tone to reinforce I should not change; "Such a good girl," she too exclaims.

Slumber parties the best, often I the guest. To friends' parents

I am "nice," a "good" friend for their daughter to know. A comfort I feel in many other homes. Not exactly at ease somewhere else, but not at peace where I live; searching for where I belong, running to where I "fit." I roll with the flow, whatever each friend wants to do; I will put their wants first, for then me they will always include.

November 2, 2014

I still wait until no time remains, not wanting you to see me pack. To pack meant I had to leave, and then you'd wonder when I'd be back. I smile at how I wasn't fooling you (or me); you sensed days prior that soon there would be days when, each other, you and I wouldn't see.

Remember when your daddy came into the house when I was leaving for the UK? Two of us, actually three of us, were certainly quite the trio that day! I was at one end of the house trying not to cry, and you at the other end, head low with saddened eyes. True to your daddy, trying to be our rock though we both know he wanted to frown too, started laughing at what a pair we were, his wife and his Roo. You and I couldn't focus on together time, apart seemed more brave; if I didn't show you my struggling heart, you wouldn't have to show me your sorrow-filled face.

I always promised you I would come back to you, good-bye was only a temporary leave. And your kiss said, "Okay, but hurry back to me please." The reunions were the best, weren't they? You sensed hours before when it was "return home" day. Certainly you felt your momma's energy erupting in eagerness

I was only hours away. Your body would twist, your short tail wag, and that light in your eyes. Both of us so excited to reunite.

Today, before leaving I ran a lap around our yard and drive, the first time I took that path since you became my Above light. I had just put clothes in the suitcase, tugged by home strings, not yet ready to leave, and as I started my run, there you were again with song for me.

In the distance, just like the mornings of our last together Earth days, the harmonic soothing call of sandhill cranes. This time you were saying, "It is okay to go; remember I am with you, you aren't going alone. Just like you carried me in your heart when traveling, I was always right next to you; I am still alongside in all that you do."

I always promised you, dear Roo, I would come back to you, it's only temporary when I leave. We both knew then we weren't apart, you and me. An invisible wire attached our heart strings. I was in tune then to the power of souls connecting even before you taught more in how to *hear* and *see*. You have taught me with more certainty that space and distance do not keep souls apart, always together heart-to-heart. Two souls on Earth or one on Earth and one above have the ability to communicate through their love.

I will be seeing a new part of the world this week; an amazing experience awaits, and I am in gratitude that beside me you are every step of the way.

November 4, 2014

I met a man who has the ability to change the world, if only his heart believed; unfortunately, his eyes see what isn't instead of possibility.

I anticipate now you are smiling, patiently listening to me; I thought I would try something new, telling you of the people I meet.

When I would return home to you we didn't relive my trips through lots of talk; I didn't recount to you my experiences or who I had added to my "scrapbook" of paths crossed. But we both knew that going away had an impact on me as your mom and as wife; I returned, better at both these roles every time. I came home having grown in reaching the center of me, more aware of who the Universe desires me to be.

Like your beautiful spirit who would scout beyond the yard's edge; entering a "zone" of doing one of the things you loved best. At times, so in your glory you wouldn't hear my voice calling to you; now I see the joy dancing in your eyes was your way of coming back to us better too.

About this gentleman I met, sharing his talent but not aware of his light yet. He plays saxophone and flute for celebrity bands around the globe, not too many more places—India, and perhaps Antarctica—left to go. He talked of Thailand, Japan, Russia, other European spots he had visited too. And China, Australia, his love of the architecture where he has visited coming through.

Initially as we talked I thought of all the lives he has touched through music that he can play; oh, what inspiration and light he can bring to each place. As he continued, I felt a lost chance to spread hope, for what he sees is how the world is greedy and in a downward slope. I anticipate he has come to forks in the road, choices to see the beauty, or to encase his soul. I tried to share my "glasses" view of the good to see. His choice not to look at gifts received.

He wasn't bitter—he had gratitude for his life; he just carried so much fear and couldn't envision helping others who experienced such strife. I am not naive to know there is a lot of pain, bigger than one person to solely bring change. But I also know if a raindrop can create a ripple that cascades to the puddle's shore, then one person can make a difference on one other, or more.

Yes, there is a certain protective coat one needs to wear; it doesn't hide one's ability to give but shelters taking on others' sorrows to bare. I anticipate this gentleman is carrying others' hurts and that explains his view; his soul has taken on other burdens that now hinder his own light to shine through.

I am grateful our paths crossed as I prepared for where my travels would take me: Israel, certainly a place that holds need. Resiliency their strength, but a need for hope too; may I bring the *lens* that helps me see *can* in my view. I will be taught, the student I know I will be; while remembering that perhaps for one, a tiny raindrop, as me.

Like your beautiful spirit who taught me to step beyond comfort's edge, to trust, to not fear, open to the chance to grow; away, only temporary, our hearts always back to where they belong—home.

Under a star-filled sky, we shared a meal and a toast, a night-time picnic, she our gracious host. Tonight, the tables adorned with silver tablecloths, grass our "floor," our walls the backyard outside their front door. Of course, baby girl, you know I felt you also enjoying this night; memory taking me back to our walks under the stars' shining light.

She not only opened us to her home and her kitchen with home-cooked food, but it was an evening shared with all of her family too. We met her husband and their three sons and two sons' girlfriends, budding love. We learned of the military education for both young men and women alike and bomb shelters as a way of everyday life. Her youngest son speaking in his native Hebrew, and yet there are Universal gestures and words that are common no matter the language used. At three years old, a "no," "mom," a high five, or a shy smile and wave of the hand; all the same whether Hebrew or American, Israel or the United States are your homeland.

Two nights before this, my meal shared with another friend, her husband, and newborn son weeks new to this life; a new restaurant, they showed me "the town," encouraging me to come back another time. Their graciousness at wanting me to experience all there was to see, my tour guides they would be. "What do I want to see? Jerusalem? More of Tel-Aviv?" And my answer, without hesitation, to experience through their eyes what means the most is best for me.

Two special evenings with two special women my hosts, who shared with me those they care about most. Graciousness, the first word to describe both; a quiet strength in one and a bolder strength in the other, both with hearts of gold. Both with a deep love for family, for friendships, and for being kind, their humbleness and resiliency, no fear, embracing what is important in life. They both work hard at career and providing for family, their balancing tightrope, their compassion, their will, their hopes.

My guardian angel, I already felt abundantly complete, gratitude for you in my life nine years, one of the most precious gifts I ever received. After these two special evenings in my time away from home, I realized even more the blessings of every soul. I have felt every person we meet is a treasure for a moment, season, or life; this trip reinforcing that to be right. I am humbled to be in the presence of Earth angels (that is exactly how I always thought of you), and am grateful for the certain ones who make me more in tune.

Each person helps me grow, but there are certain familiar ones who my heart recognizes, who my soul knows. A flutter that says, "I think we agreed, before we met, before we joined life, that someday our paths would cross at just the right time. And when our lives intersect, as we have planned it so, we will help each other on our paths to grow." So yes, Roo, once again I am coming home "better" than five days ago, another step closer to the center of my soul.

November 7, 2014

Seven races on seven continents I aspire to achieve, as you know from our runs when we would discuss the possibility. You would question Antarctica, wondering if that would be too cold, but so happy you were feeling my excitement with the goal.

It occurred to me as I watched the sun rising over the desert, a new view for a run, I may not be racing, but still progress against a dream has begun. I love how the Universe answers our prayers, wishes, and dreams; I like the surprise or the paved way for first steps, always delivering our wants and needs. I've had the chance to run in the United Kingdom, India, and now Israel too, although some was done inside at a gym, still, I ran in continents that for me are brand new.

It also occurred to me as I watched the sun greet the day, I am in a country that others perceive has an ill fate. Some people associate Israel with continuous unrest and fight, with significant historical loss, and some associate it with fright. It is easy to fear the unknown, to question what we cannot see; this week reinforced a mantra "we are not so different you and me."

After an award celebration the day prior, trays and tables filled with an array of sweets, very soon only crumbs remained, Universal the love of sugary treats. Warm smiles with hellos and feasts like a king, and of course, not long as strangers, to guests so welcoming.

I keep thinking of the Israel sunrise on my last day and the sense of peace I have similar to that "content spent" feeling after a race. As you taught me when running, how much deeper I learned perceived mountains are just hills; it struck me that this country is not "without" but stands for "I will."

I know there is always more than what we think we see, that it is usually the opposite taking place from what we perceive. One thinks another is angry and reacts in like kind, when the anger may actually be fear, furthered by panic of showing the vulnerable feeling held inside.

I didn't know what to expect when I prepared to go; I thought it would be an amazing experience, but subconsciously, did I think it militant, straight-faced, cold? Did I struggle on the drive to see brown land as far as I could see, with maybe an occasional—very occasional—hint of green? Did I somewhere deep down think they were caught in a doom loop of fighting, war, and a risk of hate? Was my lens clouded, not aware of judgment I had made?

As I watched the sun rise, its light and promise of another day we have received; it occurred to me I was surrounded by the capability to believe. The country represents perseverance and endurance; and in something much bigger, much more bold, it knows how to keep going forward in hope. I am not naive to think that there isn't sorrow too deep for some to bear; but that is part of the world everywhere. I was given the privilege to greet welcoming hands and eyes, even if that was our only way of communicating a common language of "hi."

Yes, indeed, Roo, as we both know, it is not so different wherever we may go. Some hearts have faith, some are trying to heal their pain. The land may be lush in green or lush in sand, but bonded by the same sun and moon; we are not so different each of us, me from you.

My mind caught the "almost" sentence my heart was about to say, remembering I would not be able to see you in the same way. It was my first trip returning, another *first* change; another way we need to reestablish home's base.

"I am almost home, baby girl," I would say as I made my way after each trip I'd take. I knew you could hear me, I felt excitement build into an eager rush. Your heart my pull or perhaps my heart your tug. "Soon, baby girl, soon you will see," as my heart beat to the rhythm "Hurry home, Momma, please." As I sat in the airport waiting for my next flight, I would think, "We will catch up during our run tonight." And I couldn't wait to feel my leg warmed by you as you lay next to me, our couch lounging, us and Daddy making a perfect three.

And then my ego remembered there had been a change, and my soul scrambled to ease the pain.

I was taken back to your daddy's outstretched hand, the way he gently took mine and held on tight. He was keeping me from falling off the edge, into a dark, dark night. It was the edge where my heart was deciding if I would shatter, never to be put together again; or if I would run back to where the slices and rips had deeply cut in. The rips and tears I always predicted I would feel on that day you'd whisper, "I must go." "Might as well slice off my right arm," I would tell your daddy when "someday" down the road. With his heart breaking, his pain deep, still he was my strength, his way of communicating "promise" and "always believe." Though the memory revisited on my trip home was not the easiest to replay, it started me thinking of that guiding hand's availability every day.

So many words exchanged each time he reaches out, without a word spoken out loud. Assurance, good things in our future await, new adventures, amazing memories, promise, faith. Love that grows deeper each year since "I do," I still feel like a bride twenty-one years later, nearing twenty-two. Changes, evolution, best friends, unconditional, each other's light. And that together we can enjoy and endure the ups and downs of life.

With my right arm wrapped tightly around you, I feel your imprint against me for life, I am held tightly by your daddy, his right hand intertwined in mine. I won't let go to my left, nor to my right, securely held in the middle of unconditional love on both sides.

"Soon, Momma, soon, you will see, I have been waiting for you just like past trips when you had to leave." My heart warmed by your flight across my path, my beautiful Hawk whispering, "Welcome home, so glad you're back!" Minutes later, tucked in the arm of your daddy when we hugged, securely held in the middle of that unconditional love.

My first return home since you became guardian above as a new change I embrace, it's another way I am restepping back into home as base. With your watchful eye as we went to breakfast this morning, Hawk to my right, held by Daddy's hand at my left side. Not the same way you I can now see; now more aware of each moment's miracles that reinforce believe.

November 10, 2014

It was February 10, 2013, twenty-one months to the day, when I left home for two weeks. It was the first time you and I were apart for that length of time, a first trip on my own internationally, leading others in a culture not native to mine. A first—exploring an out-of-US country by myself and getting into the routine that "Zs" don't belong when you spell. Watching football, aka soccer, chips are fries, sticky toffee pudding the best; adding "indeed," "hubby," "cheers," and "mum" to my words said.

As I walked in the door from this 2013 trip, I reflected on the two weeks that had just been. Who did they see now compared to then? Did they think I the same me? Or was I different in who they could see?

The smiling, the listening, the facilitating, the willingness to help—those traits hadn't disappeared, I knew they could tell. But did they notice that the walk was a little straighter, the head held high, that there weren't fears or "not enoughs" walking alongside? Could they see what I had declared reflected in my eyes?

Could they see the boldness that had taken place that last

day in the UK between the mirror and I? When I squarely looked at the person staring, eyes locked with mine. "I love you!" said to the one looking in turn at me, a first, a sincerity. I meant the words that sprang from somewhere deep.

You knew I came home your same momma, yet changed. And I still smile at your peek-a-boo over the end table from waiting, now time for us to play. You sensed my heart more open, my belief in *can* more pronounced and steadfast; though you knew your "job" not done, you were happy I was on this path. You had much more to teach me about letting go, trust, and unconditional love, about focusing in now and strengthening my hearing of whispers from above. We had many more miles and steps ahead to take, many more memories to store up and make.

It had been hard on both of us then to let go for two weeks, my fear creating unrest in you, your heart growing sadder as I prepared to leave. We proved a truth that we now soundly know, that prepared us for two months ago. You have to let go to grow, and the opposite of what we think is what actually takes place; apart brought me closer to home and to heart, not further away. I carried you closer when I couldn't see, and knew Daddy was also right beside me. Now it is to Daddy that I struggle to say, "See you soon, in just a few days," and it is you beside me every place.

Now on my way home, I look at the clouds down below. The ocean blue below the white, I am reminded of the vastness of life. And yet, life's oneness and connection through time and space; reminders that when we look further we are not separate but bound as one, the same.

It was February 10, 2013, twenty-one months to the day; I ponder, what will twenty-one months from now bring to mind to say? Will the walk be even straighter, the smile larger, the trust greater than today? What will I have learned even more about love, hope, and faith? Whatever it brings, I know this to be true. You will be with us, my beautiful Roo.

November 14, 2014

Maybe it was because your bed is now in front of your favorite heat source or perhaps because I still expect you to greet me when I reach the door. Maybe it was because I kept thinking of the charm hanging on my Jeep mirror, each flight toward home getting nearer. And ever my guardian angel watching out for me, together in snow and on ice, home safe we reached. Or perhaps it was because I missed our snuggles, how we would curl up at bedtime. Thus your visit in my dreams as I slept last night.

It was the sweetest dream—oh, to see your face. I held you in my arms as time stood still, did not rush away. You were asking to feel my arms wrapping you in love, and it felt so good to touch you, to hold you close. My love for you has not stopped, I know how often you are still with me; but the gift you gave me by visiting filled my heart with such joy and peace.

Daddy has placed your bed in front of the stove for warmth, and he has placed the "bridge" from the arbor to the wagon of corn. That the room would get to eighty degrees was your favorite place to sleep, and we loved how you would put your backside to the heat. As the warm air blew from the vents there you stood inches away; definitely when cold outside, in front of the corn stove a favorite place.

And the bridge, a log for the squirrels to cross, under the guise of fetching food; the reality it was a game to play with you. I haven't brought myself to clean the nose prints from the window where you stood watch, your wait for us coming home or the squirrels running across. One by one you would count as they crossed into the wagon to store up their bounty found, and when there were a few, you would let us know "now." We would open the door for your slow and steady hunt to begin, after tiptoe and low creep and crawl, your "Ready or not, here I come" would kick in.

The squirrels running back across their bridge with you leaping at their feet; sometimes you talked rather loudly to them, and they chattered back from their trees. Back inside you would come, a beeline for the stove, then after a bit, back to the window you would go. One, two, six, seven, "Hey Momma, hey Daddy, it's time," the opening of the door and back outside. Stalk, run, scurry little squirrels, bark, chatter, isn't this game fun? Such was the routine all the day long.

Maybe it was because your bed is now in front of your favorite heat source or perhaps because I expected you to greet me when I opened the door. Or maybe it was because you knew I was working from home today and would be thinking of the "now outside, now inside, now back outside" game. Or maybe it was because of the wintery cold, and we both craved the warmth of each other's love. It was the sweetest dream, the best seeing your face; I held you in my arms as time stood still, did not rush away. Through my dream, I spent an evening cradled in giving and receiving incredible love, always connected to you soul to soul.

November 16, 2014

It is the eve before a significant and treasured day, like the night before Thanksgiving or Christmas, a special holiday. Nine years ago tomorrow you came home and completed our family, you our girl, with your daddy, Hans, and me. Determined, you were wanting to curl up in my lap for the forty-five-minute drive, in your mind too far away if you were to sit beside. I tried to explain how I had gotten in trouble with a nice policeman for your brother, your Hansey, riding on my lap; yet, even then, you were nudging me there is no room for *can't*.

We made up for the moments we weren't joined as one on our drive home, that night you spread across my chest as we slept so close.

Over the past couple of days with you on my mind, I am continually thinking of our shared times. I thought of you when I heard the leaf rustle in the breeze; a rhythm like a wind chime hanging in the tree. I smiled for you had taught me how to *hear* Nature's daily talk, like when we sat outside during your final Earth walk. Being in that *now* with you taught me how to see and hear through your eyes, how we don't have to look so far ahead in our sights.

I know you had helped me increase my ability to hear long before our last days, Nature's animals and the whispers within, both avenues for what the Universe has to say. It is always easier to lean in to the messages when they are what you want to receive; it is harder when something deep knows, but the Universe opts to protect you until knowing is a need. I had sensed in the early part of the year life would know significant change, I just wasn't sure what it might be, with who—you or Daddy—but a *knowing* life would become not the same.

I listened enough to maximize time at home just us three and told the rest of me perhaps it was just imagining and change would not come to be. Though fear was continually a shadow walking next to me. You had plans, though, for me to grow, such is goodness that always comes when we are asked to let go. Now I hear in new ways, I listen to Nature speak of what may be and not just what is currently at play. Fear is no longer a partner and I learned it is safe to fall with open arms; and when you step into trust, you are given wings to keep you from harm.

I have more to learn, I know, and I am finding it magical that it is you still showing me how to grow. It is the eve before a significant and treasured day, like the night before Thanksgiving or Christmas, a special holiday. When I picked you up, I knew you were entering my world from my dreams, but I didn't begin to know just how precious the cargo, you sitting by—and lying on—me.

I brought you home to complete our family. I didn't know then you were coming home to complete me.

November 18, 2014

Running from tree to tree as if to try to keep up with us; your daddy laughing, pondering why the squirrel was in such a rush. I am certain the squirrel was following us down the drive, seeing if you in the truck he could spy. At the end of each work day—actually anytime coming home—down the driveway you would run. "Oh, Mr. Squirrel, ready or not here I come." Squirrels would run to your left and to your right, up the trees they'd go in what I am now certain was pretend fright. If one had come close enough to you, it was hard to say who was louder than who. The echo of your bark met with echoes of their chatter, each pretending to be annoyed, each acting madder.

Today's winter wonderland was the perfect memory rewind, a chance to reflect on your daily sprints down the drive. You would forge a new path through the snow, to sneak behind the garage and catch an unsuspecting squirrel the goal. We could watch them run—one, two, three, perhaps even six or eight—and we could hear you "talk tough" to them for getting away. After the game with the squirrels you would make your next rounds; birds flying in the air, you were satisfied there was nothing to be found.

The snow growing deeper beckoned me to join it in play, the ground beneath not quite ready for snowshoes, so opting for the bicycle today. I know your eyes are sparkling in laughter when my pedaling met snow extra deep; I can still see those perked ears and tilt of the head whenever curious about your momma and how silly she could be. That time you couldn't figure out why I was lying on the ground, my arms and legs moving—you had to turn around. "Momma, what are you doing?" you questioned as you nosed around me. And when I mentioned "Snow angel," you eagerly helped her halo with your feet.

I heard you encourage and remind today as I biked. "Momma, you can, don't stop, the next mile marker in sight." We proved again today that *can* is our power word and Nature, no matter the weather, a power source that fuels our spirits with peace. That together always you and I, on the trail you with me. We might have liked snuggles under blankets toasty warm, but we also enjoyed rejuvenation and "feeling alive." Such happiness we felt each time spent outside.

Today's winter wonderland was the perfect memory rewind of our joining it in play; we didn't let snow deter us, shared time and outdoors was what we craved. Now I have added bicycling to embracing winter, to join what I can't beat. Ah, yes, Roo, I hear you, and how right you are indeed. Of course, I will join it, for it is *can* that you taught me.

November 21, 2014

I am not sure if it was the article about pies that gave a nudge or my path intersecting with a nut hatch as I held it gently in my gloves.

As part of our Sunday routine, your Grandma Q highlighted an editorial for me to read. It talked of the lessons of life, learned in the art of making pies. I was taken back in time to your Grandma's special treats, but not the pies I was able to eat. The memory fondly left in storage was the homemade crust she made me, the leftover pieces made into a cinnamon delicacy. I can still see the aluminum tin plate and oh so flaky the final result that would await.

Made from so little, yet made with so much: flour, butter, sugar, cinnamon, and unconditional love. It didn't require significant money to make it an extravagant gift, yet thirty-eight years later, an imprint on me there still is. Maybe it was three crusts, or ten—I am not sure the total baked; the quantity not the impact, just one is all it would take. A gesture with the intent to give happiness, "simple" some might say. When from the heart it becomes immeasurable in the difference made.

First you sent the mourning dove to wrap me in her

message of peace, and then later in the day, a knock on the window sent me running to ensure the nut hatch still breathed.

You and I always had slightly different thoughts of how to help a bird in need; I thought help them get airborne, you thought, "Play with me." I wanted to hold them until their dazed feeling left; your instinct said let me catch them instead. We would divide and conquer in our quest to help our winged friend; me venturing outside and you cheering encouragement looking through the window from within.

Today as I held the nut hatch, I thought of yet another gift received; our memories were made not from things. Sure you liked your squeaky toys—always one tossed out of excitement before a run. And you loved your blankets; we cuddled with a variety, not just one. And you liked your coat for the snow and your red harness and matching leash, but none were essential for you to feel happy.

The rewinds in my mind, all of the moments that flash "and we have shared this too," are the times spent being together, the "simple" things we would do. We didn't need to spend money to have the best of times; let us have Nature or couch cuddles or Jeep drives. Sharing breakfasts with Daddy, making his truck front seat your own, or playing "catch me if you can" in the yard when he would get home.

I am not sure if it was the article about pies that gave a nudge or my path intersecting with a nut hatch as I held it gently in my gloves. I am certain you had a hand in both moments coming my way; that I would remember and know what you were trying to say. "Unconditional love can't be priced. Unconditional love leaves an imprint for life. What matters most comes from the heart, ensuring from each other we are never apart."

November 22, 2014

I know you are with your Hansey, how you loved your brother so; I wonder if you are also with one of my friends from long ago.

She was the black with streaks of brown-and-white version of Lassie, the collie the world knew; my friend was Peppi, not world famous, but still a jewel. We didn't run together; we didn't cuddle on the couch, for her life was outside. But she was my constant, a sureness, ever faithful, gentle, kind.

I sometimes wonder if it was you in a former life, my guardian even then watching over me all the time.

You and I both know I wasn't as aware as I am now; I didn't understand the power of soul connection to *hear* and *see*—I didn't know how. When I think of all you taught me, all you gave in unconditional love, I have moments I wish I'd given more to Peppi before she became my angel above.

"So tell her now, Mom," I hear you exclaim. "Remember, there is not distance, no separation through time and space."

My dear Peppi, with your long fur, your soulful eyes, your compassion, your gentle guide. How many times did I take you for granted? You didn't keep count. No judgment and complete acceptance is what you were about. I am in gratitude that you knew it was part of a greater plan, when we had to move to a new home without you, no joining in the van. How much love you had that you never stopped believing in me, even when I am sure it hurt your heart each other we didn't see. You stayed to guard the farm, I had to say good-bye; our times became infrequent, no longer daily in our shared time.

Even though I didn't tell you then, please know that a part of who I am today is because of who you had been. You are still with me; although I don't think I have pictures, it is you I can still see. Your beautiful long coat, your nuzzling nose. On the step where you lay watching the yard, in your mind guarding home, not demanding anything, so giving your soul.

Thank you for watching out for me, for being by my side; I hope you've rested easier sharing the "job" with others you saw join my life. I love you, Peppi, you too hold a piece of my heart, and I'm in gratitude that you have never gone far. My unassuming girl who was content to stay in the shadows waiting for our times shared, a symbol of unwavering love, always there.

You the wise soul, to be the elder watching over Hans and Roo—take care of them for me, okay? They are fortunate to be with you, for now, I know they are held safe. Your gentleness is helping Roo and me adjust to our new way of being together through space; thank you for being one of life's angels to show me the power of grace.

Okay, Rooey, be gentle with Peppi, too; remember she is older and may not be able to run and jump like you do. Gosh, why am I telling you to be gentle? I remember your care with your brother as his bones grew tired to play. You knew when it was time to sit beside and just *be* with the day.

Thank you, Roo for the nudge to talk with Peppi today. I

am sure you knew we would both find joy in connecting this way. To the moon and back, baby girl, until we talk again, and thank you, too, for taking care of a very dear friend.

November 26, 2014

Another zig and zag to our running dance. You deciding left, then right, now back and on it went. I in laughter, asking, "Time for our drunken sailor run again?" It wasn't just when leaves fell; it was also for critter chats and smells. My heart in such joy, unknowing of where but letting you lead the way; certain whatever path, you were keeping us safe. Flexibility, trust, enjoying every step one takes, regardless of weather, regardless of terrain.

You and the Universe have again been speaking with me, reminders of the power of life if we stay open to see. It first came in the form of rain and wind and an umbrella that inverted more than once. Not sheltering the elements of the air but most certain handing out laughter to some.

You kept me laughing at what a sight I must be, and instead of willing it to my way, I chose to smile in glee. I was reminded of the times you and I would run despite rain. "Trees are shelter," I would exclaim. With our eyes sparkling and our heads held high, we would run as if it was full sunshine (of course, it was in our hearts and minds). With that same spirit, as you would expect of me, in this windy rain I walked, no umbrella did I need.

Trust we will be led, always, to exactly where we should be, just as you always zigzagged us to our Jeep. I had an errand to do, a task to complete, but the location not yet open, service delayed for the need. Some might see it as a roadblock, a plan derailed, a hurdle they didn't need; I knew I was being redirected, asked to trust and be patient, a whisper, "In time, just wait and see."

Another location, unplanned treasures found to take, a wonderful exchange of conversation, a pay-it-forward kindness, hugs exchanged. The treasures holding symbolism of how you now soar and gratitude that earlier I encountered a closed door. I was led to right where I needed to be, affirmation of the power when we trust, when we believe.

Today, you knew I needed an extra nudge of what I know; such is the Earth journey when our souls are stretched to grow. We can feel strength, be soul connected, then old habits or grief stop by; thank you for being certain I listened as you sent messengers of flight.

The swans, the blue birds, the cardinal, and the turkey too, all divinely whispering reminders of what I knew. I am certain it was all who played a part in my run today, but I know it was especially the bluebird and what it had to say. With a happy heart and joy in each step made, I zigged and zagged as I ran today.

But as if the turkey's reminder of my blessed life was not enough, nor the smile forming as I thought of our "drunken sailor" route, you nudged me, "Not here, keep going, follow." And then there you were, slightly ahead, yet magnificently beside me. There, as beautiful Hawk for me to see. Like the leash that attached our steps, our hearts entwined for life;

affirmation of what I know, no space, never good-bye.

Some might see roadblocks, a hurdle they didn't need. Or they might not hear the whisper, "Not here, keep going, let me lead." You taught me to be joyful, to trust, to love the zig and zag, to be open to what we might see. I now understand just how powerful the message you were giving me. Had I stopped where I planned and not let go, I would have missed the flight with you today, affirmation for my soul. I was led to right where I needed to be, affirmation of the power when we trust, when we believe.

November 28, 2014

It was a kick in my stomach when into it reality sank; accidentally all of the texts erased. You had been whispering, "Time
for new, you won't lose me." Now, getting my attention more
boldly you decided to speak, "Mom," as you more gently say,
"it is time to look in different ways."

Perhaps because words are how I connect heart and soul,
or perhaps because I revere each moment in which a miracle
I still hold. Moments that embrace, define, expand awareness,
shift, and change, I want to keep close, stay with, secure in
place. Recognizing the power of what took place, the impact,
the difference it has made; I don't see where I could be hindering purpose and faith.

I am so held in the comfort of all that was, the warmth of
each moment, the safety of what I've been taught. But I short-
change trust when I waver in knowing that moments are never
lost.

The imprints are with us for life; what matters most stays
by our side. As I have been walking down the lanes of memories recent and long ago, you keep whispering with each one
shown. "This happened to make you who you are, and this—see

how it still rests softly on your heart. The moments that stung were precious gifts as you now see, and other moments prove always believe."

No more within reach, the fear you were now further away, with the texts now all erased. All of the conversations with your daddy during our last together Earth days—I knew it wasn't good-bye in your message of "Time for a new slate." It was the opposite: "Time to open to the new that awaits." You know my dreams—we talked at length about them, I know— and you told me you would help me achieve them. That is why you had to go. And now, I hear you as you say, "All that I taught you won't go away. You will take me forward with you in the steps made. Let's help the world see beauty, hope, and faith, that there is no distance through space."

In breakfast cooked at home, a first time in weeks. In the lengthier snuggles in bed, your daddy and me. The moments of you I still trace in all I do, but I am trusting I can keep them and also embrace the new. It is what you expect for me to best honor the gift of you.

As you have nudged me with this most recent lesson—still, and always, you teach—true to you, affirmation powerfully brought to me. I had heard the call twice, and then in flight a visit near me: "Hello, Owl, I am filled with gratitude that again we meet."

"See, Mom, always, never apart, the imprint of the day we watched Owl will always remain in your heart. And when you asked me to come the week after I went above, as Owl I reminded you of my love. And today, I came to praise how you continue to hear what I and the Universe say, how I am always near. You weren't expecting Owl, a beautiful and awe-filled surprise, the power of staying open to what is yet to be in life.

Like the squirrel that I showed you jumping in a leap of faith, let's go forward together and help bring positive change. To the moon and back our love, with you always, I am right here above."

In awe at what again you have brought my way, this time from beautiful Owl and your message of faith.

Mile after mile further I run from me

A tenderness in her eyes unlike anyone else whose eyes look at me. A readiness to put herself second if she can fulfill my needs. A safety net when I actually talk of what saddens or angers my heart; always ready to dry tears and encircle me in her arms. With an all-consuming love and gentleness as if I might break, messages when I will soon be out of her sight: "Stay safe." I have her faith in who I am, in who I will grow up to be. And inside, where she can't see, I wrap my heart in a protective coating. I cannot accept unconditional love, for I am not worthy, I am not enough.

I must cross in front of it to get to my room. For the few seconds it takes, I block the view. "Hey, don't block the TV," the words resonate. Though I run faster, still I hear, "You are in the way." I stay in my room longer, or I wait for his sleep. Other options that minimize me being seen. If I must cross the path when he is wide awake, on my knees to crawl under the screen is the approach I take. Perhaps I am still visible, but I am small and not what catches the eye; what is better to watch is the TV in full sight.

December 1, 2014

The circle has traveled a full three hundred and sixty degrees, grateful I am that this time I am not in retreat. I was tempted, as I know you talked me through; it felt easier, in the spirit of simplicity, but we both know that wasn't the truth. A few years ago, when I was traveling to that peel-every-layer-back core of me, I did not have energy, nor desire, for a Christmas tree. Depression was stronger than my will to celebrate, darkness the preference over the season's magical ways. Then so lost, so far from "home," finding the only refuge I could in the depths of my soul. This time, when I briefly thought this year I might forego, you reminded me that I would be taking the wrong approach.

A few years ago, the tree too bright, certain ornaments held memories I couldn't bear to see. Each ornament wanted to shine "you are not worthy." The child "not enough" was the adult feeling the same. Consumed by it, yet I tried to run from the pain. "I have failed, I was failing, I have always failed," the words repeating; I was running from, to run right into, the unraveling memories. The child who felt "less than" had to give the adult permission to let go. The adult had to learn self-acceptance and that pain was part of growth. The ornaments were a reminder of what couldn't yet be embraced—that every single moment in life has purpose, and we have choice in the perspective we take. Just as Christmas contains hope and wishes of peace, now I am starting to say, "Thank you" to the younger me. All that was experienced led me to who I now am; able to keep my heart open though physically seeing you I can't.

I thought about the ornaments we hung last year—more than objects for they carry memories held dear.

The promise of endurance, that abundance is in less, blessed with a mom who has always strived to make each Christmas the best. When I did not yet know at one year of age, on Christmas Eve, her last dollars she gave. Home with a tree and ornaments to complete, these tiny shimmers now find a place on her children's trees. Every time I take each one from its safe holding place, I reflect on the sturdiness, forty-six years without break. I can *see* my mom lovingly making Christmas home, as I hang on the tree the memory of hope, a richness in simplicity, a sureness of unconditional love.

A soldier made from a clothespin and a doll of blue yarn, school bazaars, elementary age, the chance to shop for presents to give. If only I could recall what I purchased yet still remember the excitement in finding "perfect" gifts.

We couldn't forget to put the green reindeer on a branch, your daddy's childhood ornament, also from long ago past. And of course his first stocking, smaller than your paw in width and height, and I am still impressed that the trim is not too "unwhite." Forty-four years old that tiny stocking, another object that speaks much; I anticipate his parents would talk of how fast time goes, its incredible rush.

Of course there are our name ornaments: "Pete," "Chris," "Hans," and "Roo," and I know you have seen the precious one your Aunt J'fer just made of you. There is a memory tapping on my shoulder of the ornament with my name, and how we came to get your daddy's, my search trying to make them the same. As a little girl I felt left behind, my parents on a trip I was not allowed to join. True to your Grandma Q., a gift she brought back to me. That blue ornament with my name etched in white, every year since, it joins the tree. Your daddy took me to the place I couldn't go to as a kid, and a blue ornament with white lettering now also his. This year when I hang our named ornaments on the tree, I will no longer think of the child in me. If that child had any emptiness to fill, I can assure her that she is now complete: family, blessings, finding love as I near the center of me.

This week we will decorate the tree together as we did last year. I will just be listening differently for you to whisper, "Hang this one here." And as I take each one from its box to find where it should hang, I will be in gratitude for the memory that each one contains. Like each chapter of my life that I now fill with experiences new, the ornaments are a foundation for where I've been—I am now in gratitude. I don't know all that you and I might ponder as we decorate future trees, but I am most certain—new ornaments there will be. The foundation will expand; life is about evolving. More memories will influence and shape. Thank you, my beautiful baby girl as I know you will continue to show me the way.

December 5, 2014

The nest more visible with each dropping leaf, now the branches bare, the haven fully seen.

I wonder where our Robin is now; if she is still nearby, or if she has started south. I think of her often, a kindred soul; both of us knowing what it was to let our children go.

As you have always known when you watched my heart grow content, the time from September through December is a favorite. Some find it an ending, as the leaves turn and fall; trees become empty, longer darkness, wishes that the timing for winter stalls. For me, I find it a season of hope, that in the changing landscape, transformation unfolds.

A dear friend instilled in me a tradition on my birthday: "What have you learned in the past year?" I think that reflection actually begins as winter draws near. As the trees begin to show more of the sky and their neighboring trees, I find it is my heart that opens more to what I can see. As the ground shifts in layers, blanketed for the grasses to stay warm, I too am shifting, shaping, further defining in form.

The woods grow quiet as summer visitors prepare to hibernate, a stillness takes hold, time to pause, to wait. I too, feel the pull to stand still, that I may further *see* and *hear*, my heart beating an excitement for what lies ahead in the new year.

For some time, the reoccurring scene had played in my mind, the orange, purple, and red hues of the sky. Mountains beside me, walking across that plain; the setting sun glowing across my cheeks, shining across my upturned face. Being cheered on to keep walking toward a large cliff, a wide span; I wasn't yet there but I could see from afar where the edge began. I was not afraid each time the replay, like Robin's babes I felt safe. I now know that I was being led to take a leap of faith and that the edge I would stand at was the life course I would face.

Now the branches bare, this haven fully seen, like the edge of that cliff, my heart still beats. The promise you made of what you will still teach me from above, that by trusting and letting go, even more I will grow. I am quiet now, as I start to slowly run through this change with you, held in the comfort that if I allow, you will bring things anew. I no longer walk the mountainous plain, for I stepped off the edge into open sky, and right beside me you remain, always by my side.

December 7, 2014

Tucked away, hidden, safely held in the recesses of the drawer and in my mind; I hadn't remembered this I would find.

My first thought was even then, I was destined to love souls with four legs, my destiny with you. And then I remembered what else this little bundle would do. Tucked in the corner of my pillowcase each night when I slept, watching over me, keeping me safe, comforted in my rest. I don't remember the exact fears the little girl in me felt, but with this tiny stuffed dog in its love I was held.

Perhaps it is part of the process as each year draws to a close. Or maybe it is my sister's upcoming wedding that stirs a review of how time goes. And I am certain it is also because my heart has opened wide, so much I am hearing and seeing with you now a different angel guide.

Nudged to revisit the past in memory and in collected physical things, with encouragement to let go and allow new entering. Sometimes it is a recollection of a moment in time, where hurt, fear, or "not enough" were the themes I tried to hide. With the gift of learning there's always more than what we see, I am now able to understand more from *then* and find peace. With the gift of your unconditional love that aided in me finding love of me, I am able to thank that little girl within for her experiences that helped who I've come to be.

Sometimes it is picking up or reading a physical item that has been kept and not released—as if it still contains the moment that made it an item to keep. As I hold on to it, I hear the whisper, "It is time and it is okay," and then I hear, "Trust, imprinted for life, make way." I have come to trust that which matters never leaves, stamped forever in our heart to draw upon when we need. Perhaps it is also because of where you led me to, my beautiful life teacher, my baby girl, Roo.

Who I am is "more than enough," I now see. I have found the ability to start loving me.

Some things held on to for they contained that which wrapped me in love, during a time I was trying to prove to myself I was enough. Some memories held on to for I feared revisiting the pain; was I strong enough to go back and face? With your continued love in the messengers you send to me, I have been able to keep revisiting and then release.

No exception when after I had purged the *old* and found this little buddy tucked away, you sent two signs across my path to affirm you and how I'd spent my day. A feather on my run and a Hawk as I biked our trail and the whisper, "So proud of you, keep listening, keep going, you will not fail."

Tucked away, hidden, safely held in the recesses of my heart, I am learning what I can let go of and what I know will never part. This little bundle I will keep—I think this one is meant to travel life with me. So small in size, yet it keeps taking on more as I add new significance to it and what it stands for. Now it holds safely this time with you and continues to watch over all that I do.

Until I find you again, little one, at just the right time, stay warm and safe nestled in the corner of my life.

December 11, 2014

This tenderness washes over him, and you can see the warmth of his soul. I have always said, "Children and animals love him so."

I watched moments with a newfound friend—comical to watch this pal's face, "That is the spot, don't stop," followed by a raised leg. The tail, stubby, but still great in its talk of joy, and your daddy's laughter knelt beside this four-legged boy. I have always loved to watch this side of your daddy, his compassion for children in fur coats; a cat or a dog no partiality, except you who he loved most.

Sometimes, these moments bring reflection of your grandpa—not your daddy's dad, but mine; you may have met once or perhaps twice. Or maybe you spend time with him now as I know he spends time with your brother Hans, who I am certain you have found. Anyway, your grandpa also loved what us humans call dogs; always had one as a companion, his truck seat tag-a-long.

As I continue to dance with past memories, many coming into view, I continue to increase awareness of what I am being led to. I am being led to those moments that left a mark, which may be holding me back from new starts. I am being asked to walk back to what took place, to watch the rewind and see in a different way. I am being asked to remember what the younger me felt, to apply understanding, to see there is more to what these memories held.

We learn through opposites, precious gifts one soul gives for another to receive; and we are also often more alike than not, if we step back from ourselves and choose to see. A little girl who felt she wasn't enough as his daughter; he too, did not believe he was good enough as her father. The walls grew higher, the searing against self-esteem deep, the reality that one's self pain was begetting the same, a purpose to break a cycle it would leave.

A mother who internalized "you are not enough" passed her pain to her son; internalizing the same pattern, he was unable to change his feelings of nonlove. He was not able to see that his mom's soul had a wish, that he would break a cycle in how he would live. His pain too great, not strong enough to break free, passed on his pain to his daughter, passed on to me.

My purpose was to step away from his shadow, to be strong enough for us both, to believe the mirror reflection when it whispers, "More than beautiful to behold." Baby girl, you entered my life here on Earth when the journey to the center of me was about to begin, that you would teach me to open my heart, to unfold in my belief within. You, so instrumental in teaching me that in order to be unselfish, you have to be yourself; that honoring who you are ensures that the reason for crossing paths with another is upheld. If I hold back a portion of me, I've shortchanged the planned Divine appointment when another I should meet.

In my mind, I see a drafting compass, the first dot of the

circle the day the letter received; the day his internal pain erupted, the day our relationship severed and I chose to start looking for me. His soul giving me the ultimate unconditional love, though both of us as humans would feel it a substantial price until we understood what unconditional was. Twenty-one years later, the circle has made its way around, nearing the completed loop; the healing about to take place when my sister says "I do." I, her matron of honor, in love with my life, my husband, and me; no longer the bride loving life and her husband, yet desperately seeking acceptance, to be "enough" in what her father sees. All who witness to my sister saying, "yes" will carry abundant love, including our dad, witness from above.

I know he will be smiling at the beauty of my sister radiantly in love, proud of his family, of the adults his daughters have become. His heart overflowing, his soul whispering, "She heard, she chose well, she fulfilled our agreement perfectly." The cycle broken, replaced by the ability to give and receive unconditional love abundantly. His soul no longer in pain, her heart now free, for she now knows she is "more than enough," his daughter, me.

December 12, 2014

"I see the moon, and the moon sees me," I couldn't help thinking tonight's shape a wink.

As I was driving to the Christmas dinner, there it was in the night; the silo star in full light. Earlier in the week, I was nostalgically missing that beacon around the curve, its familiar shine awaiting the turn. Its light a promise of what time would soon bring: the countdown from December 1 to Christmas Eve. It wasn't lit as December knocked, and two weeks in, still a dark spot, I felt it was a sign, it was time to let go; in with the new, time to evolve from the old. Across the street, a different star to shine bringing sureness and peace with that light.

You and the Universe continue to show me that you hear, always responding to my requests, ever near. I like to refer to them as miracle moments that are affirmations to believe; some might call them ordinary, or they might not even see. It can be a wish for a parking space nearby; as I near, one opens up at that exact time. Or it may be a request for more or less time, a meeting postponed, or no wait in line. Or it is a wish that a feather from you I would see, shortly after one found at my feet.

Frequently the moments when you and the Universe let me

know your love for me, and often you confirm I am right in what I hear and see. You, my teacher in how to hear what isn't voiced out loud for the human ear, yet when we are still, the guidance is so very clear. Yesterday no different, you whispered to me, "Mom, know how each time we walked or ran together you would review the day? You would always get to an 'ah-ha,' as you used to say. We talked without words you would speak; I would hear your voice through your heartbeat. I know we are learning how to communicate through space, and it takes time to adjust to this new way. But part of the gift I wanted to give you—and the way you said you could honor me and fulfill your purpose too—was to write so that others would find hope, love, and faith. When their hearts were grieving they could still see beauty and grace."

I had let go of the familiar silo star, another gift you gave me to trust letting go no matter how hard. Seeing that new star in its brightness, I knew it was your message that I had heard you right. I was willing to let go of "old" habits so as to allow for the new. Just like you are even stronger beside me now when I trusted then to let go of you.

Perhaps you thought I needed another sign, or you wanted to send extra love on this day. (It's been twelve weeks since you became my guardian because you could not stay.) Or maybe, because you know how my heart beats, you are getting as excited as me in how we are growing in our ability with each other to speak. As I draft thoughts to prepare to write, you send an e-mail your daddy has awaited for some time. Another shipment for his car restoration is on its way, just like when you sent parts two other times in those last days.

"I see the moon, and the moon sees me." I couldn't help thinking tonight's shape a wink. "Hello, baby girl, I love you too." To the moon and back, my Roo.

December 16, 2014

"Our hearts are very old friends" wrapped in tissue paper due to their delicacy and the new address I had on my list of needs. Another extraordinary moment as I define, affirmation from above at just the right time.

Grief knocked again on Sunday, and what I know at the soul level temporarily stepped aside. The most wonderful two days in celebration of my sister's marriage yet sorrow burrowed into crevices of my mind. What I needed most now that the fifteen-month planning had crested to complete— the security of home to take away the void I now felt in me. Like Christmas, a birthday, or a vacation we eagerly await, then feel a little sad when what we anticipated for the future are now memories already made. Joy for my sister and the brother-in-law I have gained; but you, my Roo, not there to greet us when home we came.

I was reminded when walking in the door, home is not yet feeling that familiar secureness and warmth.

I had on my list of things to do, reaching out to a friend for her new address now that she had moved. In that Divine way that you help the Universe answer my needs, in the mail a package for me. My True North friend, as we consider each for the other to be, sent a perfect gift describing our friendship, with her new address, at the right time as a reminder to pause and breathe. As you know baby girl, your momma has been working on learning to "let go of the reins" and trust all things work out as they are meant to. This package yet another "miracle" moment of how the Universe always comes through.

But once I open the door a crack to let sadness visit me, another partner to sadness tries to take a seat. How quickly one's foundation can teeter and sway, fear of not being enough trying to erode faith. My dear girl, you my teacher of self-worth because you loved me so, why is it that every once in a while there is still the old patterns trying to take hold? The mirror that usually reflects *can* is still draped with a cover so as to see remnants of *can't*. Today continued to test whether I would choose to trust in who I am and in what I have come to know. Or would I first utilize the old mirror that says, "Self, still a ways to go."

As I started my run, I felt you beside me; I knew the wind blowing against us was your way of saying, "Forward, trust, believe." And then as quickly as the wind threatened a "perfect storm," no longer a breeze mounting intensity to build in damaging form. My hope and faith elevated, my heart opening back up to possibility, seeping back in is trust in the Universe and trust in me.

Now that you had my attention, you wanted to make sure my soul recognized how the heart beats best; as your daddy and I are heading back home, above us a fall from its nest. You sent a young owl for me to know you're always with me and wisdom's there for me to hold. In my hands I gently picked it up, its heart now at rest. On a bed of leaves I bid it peace, its imprint felt on my fingers long after it had given me its best. A sacrifice so that I might *see*, to regain my wisdom in trusting that space does not separate you from me.

It only takes a moment to gently take our hand and guide us back to our destined path. In the book *True North* by Bill George, True North is "our orienting point that helps us stay on track." "Our hearts are very old friends" wrapped in tissue paper due to their delicacy; and the new address now complete from my list of needs. Owl for me to hold ever so gently; your message, "Momma, always trust, always believe." Extraordinary moments as I define, affirmation from above at just the right times.

December 18, 2014

"I am uncomfortable, and that is a good thing," a dear friend expressed to me, her wisdom that we are growing when we are not at peace.

If we feel unsettled, we have two choices to make; we can avoid it or it we can face. We can fight it and strive to hold on to control so very tight, or we can stand still, let go, allow, trust all to be all right.

I too feel uncomfortable, caught between the "old" and the "new," not fully certain of what exactly I should do. On one hand, I stand in excitement of what I cannot yet see, and on the other, I am holding on to what has brought contentment for me. An e-mail from your Grandma Q. offering a different plan, she could host Christmas if I felt this year I can't. If we can't physically see you, her fear Christmas would be sad; hosted at her house, keep it simple, each of us bring a dish to pass.

My immediate response, to keep our tradition the same; feeling if I don't, home that I had come to embrace will continue to slip further away. A tiny voice within asks, "Did you answer 'I will' because you are holding on to the feelings of Christmas when Roo you could physically see? Or do you truly want to make, bake, and host; to fill your home with your family?"

Pondering Christmas was the catalyst to move me into *uncomfortable* for the day, touching that part of my heart that tries to quietly lay. Skilled and trained in controlling feelings through control of plans; no room for fear of change or for the reality of feeling sad. If Christmas isn't at home, am I embracing the new? Or am I running from sorrow and the process of *going through*? Do I need to keep it at our house so that I learn to build home in new ways? Or if keeping it at home, am I holding back from change?

Just as we did whenever I was not at one with the day, to the trail for a bike ride that certainty would find its way. In the quietness of the night, clarity; I only need to focus on right where I am at, and just *be*. I pedaled through the darkness, only seeing a few feet in front of me; feeling safe, starting to partner with peace. Another experience learning trust, the lesson twofold: I don't need to see far ahead, the other, faith of the soul.

Christmas will be at home with your Grandpa and Grandma Q., your Aunt J'fer, Uncle Kevin, and I know you will join us too. If I have a moment where sadness knocks at the door, I will remember that you are watching from above. And I will remember how you taught me the most incredible unconditional love. I will remember what you want for your daddy and I. To fully, in all of its uncomfortable stretching, be joyful in our lives.

December 20, 2014

"Go to the trail today, Mom, for your run" you whispered to me. "The road's not where you need to be."

I have started limiting my routine to a roadside view, perhaps subconscious that on the trail I will miss you. That is part of my learning, I know—how to trust the permanence of imprints while learning to also let go.

As I started my run, you knew what I needed to see: footprints in the snow offering to lead. Not coincidence I know, that they were alongside the distance I had planned; your way of ensuring I felt you holding my hand. I ran with the mantra, "in the now of this run" and sentence two, "in gratitude for your abundant love." You have always smiled at the mantras that I repeated in my mind; matching with the miles my feet, harmony in rhythmic time.

You also knew before me what this run would mean; as I neared the end, another release of grief. I felt them start at the core when I reached the parked truck, and I wasn't able to reach down to unhook your leash so you could jump. I wasn't able to open the door for you to enter first, nor give you water from our special bowl to quench any thirst. I could feel you under the pines, right next to me, but I longed to physically touch you—those brown soul-filled eyes I longed to see.

"Tears are to the soul what soap is for the body," a proverb that came to mind; and the tears, the love-full, sorrow-filled, healing tears from deep inside. "I love you so much, baby girl," my voice saying aloud, and your assurance as you whispered, "Let the tears pour out." You also whispered, "Mom, somewhere out there is a four-legged babe who feels not enough and you and Daddy must help him through, just as I helped you, Mom, find enough in you. I am not going anywhere, Mom, that you know and trust; I will help you find the ability to bring in new while keeping the bond of us."

What I also love, my beautiful Roo, is how you work with the Universe to help me through. You knew you could validate what I heard you say by sending me an animal message in a familiar way. As I started the to-do list I had for a day at home, that knock on the window calling my soul. Outside to rescue a feathered friend, to hold it in my hand until its heart beats again. A titmouse with the most watchful eye, with my hand I started to gently lift, then immediately it soared high.

Its message of healing and balance just for me, always baby girl your message, "Hope, love, believe."

December 21, 2014

Sometimes my will would try to make it your will. After all, Mom knows best, right? You, more focused on our run and the sights, telling me you weren't thirsty this time. Other times, you would challenge me to a game of jumping rope with your leash as you decided you just might.

Something inanimate, yet it speaks volumes to me, today's reminders of our daily running. That old-fashioned water pump that replenished many a thirst, my arm pumping until out came water in a cold burst.

Yet again, you saw my torn heart wonder, is it time? Or too soon to find? Each push of the pedal and shift of gears, and I am thinking time is drawing near. Mixed emotions, would I want this to be the one? Or was it too soon, the lessons without you not yet done?

As I left this pump, a restorer of a sustenance to life, you sent me Cardinal in its radiant flight. Its whisper of "joy" and "vibrantly be," there to remind me to lessen the seriousness settled tightly around me.

True to you and the Universal love, now that I had listened, you'd continue to speak from above. With a lighter heart, I continued with the ride, reminded of the miracle moments in life. With the lens I look through shifting, regrouping, remembering my foundation of faith, I posted another inspirational message: gratitude for a rosy-cheeked cool-weather day. Just as I put a positive energy into the world with the hope it would pay joy forward too, there you came in the tree, Hawk whispering, "Proud of how you *hear*, love to you."

With my eyes and ears now open, trusting what is meant to be, your daddy and I toward foster care for the three of us to meet. We heard the familiar "horse" sound of four feet across the floor; or our hearts heard what we remembered when you would come for home's door. The door opened, and out he energetically, full-force leaped; as your daddy later said, it wasn't you running to me.

As Daddy said to my flood of tears, our home has known Hans and you for over twenty-one years. Now home empty, matching the erratic beat of our hearts; me still waking up every couple of hours, listening to make sure you aren't far. I wanted to have our home filled back up with…you.

My answer provided as I cried—it is still too soon.

And thank you again, my dear Roo, as your daddy and I went for our relaxing drive. There in the tree, Hawk whispering, "Always with you, by your side."

December 22, 2014

Did she know the responsibility she was being asked to bear?
That I was asking this of her, was I being fair?

For her it was new scenery, a new experience, a chance to
do something she is good at, something she loves to do. For
me, familiar landscape, something I also enjoy, but should I
consider it new?

The connection to my waist so as not to experience arm
pull—new. (I couldn't share your red harness, nor red leashes,
safely tucked away what you used to use.) The pace, the curiosity, the things that drew her attention left and right, not the
same, as she and I ventured down the trail tonight.

My "niece" with four legs, my first time with a running
mate since you and I found partnership in a new way. You by
my side, now watching over two, whispering encouragement
to Daisy to quickly learn what to do. Always, still, your unconditional love, sent to me from your guardianship above.

She did well for her first time, of course that you knew. For
you were answering my request—I needed help to get through.
It was not a request made just moments before Daisy and I
intertwined leashes to begin; it was at the start of the day when

I was unable to get to my "in-tuneness" within. I knew you and the Universe would bring me the clarity with which to *see*, your gentle nudge throughout the day "try to run with her, have Daddy help, try with little Daisy."

Not two years old yet, but already a wise soul; that her purpose was to make me smile, laugh, and have happiness take hold. You had sent the deer this morning to speak to me, their message of gentle determination, compassion, love, and peace. As is often so, messengers come in premonition of what I can't yet see, their "toolkit" for life guiding me in how to be. You wanted me the teacher for Daisy, to remember this was her first time and to make sure compassion for her, and for self, remained first to mind.

One of our memories, this picture I captured then safely tucked away. I liked it for the shadows at play. Since dusk was carrying nighttime, a shadow I could not see, but I knew you still encouraged us, for the rain you helped ease. On my drive home, knowing I was going to try, I had made yet another request, if the rain didn't or did let up, it was a sign.

Only sprinkles when getting home; Daisy and I were meant to go.

One more step in honoring you; to give and to be open to receiving, is what you want me to do. A dear friend said today how her cousin felt recently filling her home with four legs again; her angel above was her "baby," this one by her side a dear girlfriend. You, a best part of me. I know you are gently encouraging me to enjoy running companionship with a "niece."

She embraced the new, knowing she had a special task to complete, through her trust and her willingness, forward she helped lead. Thank you, Daisy for your gentle and strong way; I am in gratitude for your leap of faith. Trust begets trust. Hearts have a way they just know, you, special friend, with your healing soul.

December 24, 2014

Christmas Eve has started to knock, its daylight not yet arrived, my mind, my heart, seems to be ignoring the time. It is a pattern that has formed, routine waking throughout the night, but usually it is brief, only a fleeting moment of open eyes. I have thought it you that I am waking for, just as the countless times you whimpered, "More." When you were cold, you would call out, "Covers please," or your head nestled on my shoulder, in the crook of my neck, your warm breath in sleep.

Two-thirty is giving way to three-thirty, and I ponder what has me fighting peace, that I can't get back to the gentleness of sleep. I wish it was an excitement for Christmas, the eagerness like a child anticipates Santa and sleigh; but my mind isn't even thinking of the upcoming day. It keeps thinking of New Year's Eve and what stage will be set for 2015.

There is an excitement within, for what lies ahead I cannot yet see, but it isn't anticipation that has replaced sleep. Do I fear newness that I also crave? I can sometimes see myself standing between two doorways. One represents what is and who I know to be, the other what will teach and continue to evolve me. No, I don't think that is why I am now nearing four o'clock, and still my eyes open wide, not yet letting go, the "ah-ha" I hope to find.

As daylight draws nearer, I think I am awakening to *it*. A significant reason I resist. If New Year's comes without a four-legged companion in our lives, I am afraid the year will carry a tone of emptiness at our side. I am already clutching to what might have made home feel like home because you aren't here. I am not ready to begin without you in a new year.

A rain in the night begins to soothe me; my heart slows, incoming an ease. There is the rain soothing me again, taking me back to then. I hear you as I heard your assurance during our last together Earth days. "Mom, you know there is never good-bye, nor distance, nor space." The rain falls to the rhythm of peace, reminding me that still you will be with me experiencing all of the year's new things. Together the weather and I cleanse as I match the rain with my tears, washing away the pain and the fears.

Sleep is knocking, as the new year awaits, restored to my foundation trust, hope, faith.

December 25, 2014

At least twice I have thought I need to watch where I set these—the stocking stuffers that include chocolate you can't eat. And then I remember you aren't physically here to think our stockings should also be yours; that the Chex Mix, the sugar cookies, the Christmas brunch you wouldn't be asking for. Tears held back as the void made itself visible where family had been, incompleteness knocking, home feeling like a house again. The new throw blanket my comfort and my curse too; today, lounging on the couch under a throw wouldn't include you.

Awake from a nap, back to the familiar pages of pictures, almost a frantic peruse, the return of anxiousness to find the one to choose. When the silence is the loudest, my patience the least, trust absent that we will be led to the one to share in mutual need. I know I want to adopt one who will come to feel how it is more than enough, recognizing that it will be your daddy and I who will gain immense love.

In my quest, I hear the whisper, "The time is not yet." Reminded of advice I gave a dear friend. "If you are wanting it so desperately, you are trying to rely on another to fill a hole within; let go of the urgency. When you no longer feel the intense need then time to begin." I know I am trying to rush through the uncertainty, to control what I want to be. I hear the whisper, "Trust, be patient, stay open to possibility. Be with every moment, and don't worry of the next; let go and let us, the Universe, take care of the rest."

It has only taken two days to let in a sliver of love for another that has four running feet; now our fourth day my focus on another who is equally eager to see me. With my "niece" Daisy excited and happy to be my running mate, your daddy takes us for a three-mile escapade. Daisy, free from her fenced home, giving her gratitude to me in the form of hope.

As we ran to our halfway mark, hope, peace, and trust slowly filling my heart. Ahead, I could see the deer cross our path, further reinforcing their message: allow gentleness to take my hand. We stopped, and right on cue, you knew what I needed, my beautiful Roo. You called to me through the trees, "Stillness, Mom, and you will see. Mom, beside you I will never leave." Owl echoing its hoot hoot hoot, tears instantly flowing my gratitude. Out loud my voice, "Baby girl, I love you so," and instantly you respond through a second hoot hoot, "I know."

As Daisy and I started back, for daylight was getting weary from a busy day, you called a third time, "Listen to what she has to say." In your hoot, "I love you, Mom, and I am here for you; I am guiding Daisy to help you through." With her grab at the leash, pausing to play, Daisy whispering, "Lightheartedness and allow the surprise of each day."

Once again I am reminded it is the lens through which I see; right next to me you are, and will always be. I don't need to worry about what tomorrow will bring; in every moment I am always given exactly what I need. Those that I need and those that need me will be brought to my life path exactly when they should be. This includes two legged and four legged—it includes the one to make home meaningful again; in the meantime, I will enjoy my newfound friend.

December 26, 2014

Another first this year, the day after Christmas, our tree; I do not want to keep it up this time through New Year's Eve. Perhaps it is the craving for open space, that clogged corners hinder entry of new ways. Or perhaps it is wanting simplicity back, that there only needs to be one or two things for impact. Or maybe it is the restlessness following me through, that isn't finding coziness in the Christmas-lit room. Gratitude for the whisper, "No need to explain why. Just keep doing what your heart feels is right."

As I ran again with Daisy, each of us fulfilling our purpose to give what the other needs, my restlessness quieted, my emptiness subsided, my heart embracing peace. A few extra minutes cuddled with Daisy before it was time for me to leave, I was reminded of the power of stillness, of being, the ability to hear heartbeats. Daisy and I are moving each other forward, tomorrow we can't see; her teaching me all that matters is right now, enjoying what life brings. Daisy has a wisdom, a confident strength; she embraces where she is at with unwavering faith. "We have found each other," I whisper, "to help each other," into her ear I say, and her kisses affirmation she feels the same way.

On the way home, the majestic sunset in my view, to my right, flying in parallel is you. Majestic Hawk for the fourth time on this day when I am in need: your message, "Keep going, I am with you, I am proud of your ability to *see*. You may be hurting, but you have courage to stay open and unfold, I'm always with you, loving you, you are never alone." My dear Roo, an angel of the Universe, rallying others to love me through, to the moon and back, always my love for you.

December 28, 2014

My favorite scene, when he rides his mountain horse over the ravine. A leap of faith, what no one else would dare try, his trust in his horse and himself that all would be all right.

The Man from Snowy River revisited in place of sleep; perhaps it was my spark of courage, the reminder of trust I, too, did need. The movie as messenger for the change we have put into motion, for our own leap. The cliff drawing closer— one, two, three.

The blanket and pillows that have stayed on your couch, the blankets and one of your beds in front of the fire where you lounged. It is time to wash the blankets and let go of your bed. Our upcoming new family member needs her own to lay her head.

I hold each close to my face, no longer detecting your smell as a trace. I hear you whisper, "Trust that though altering where I once lay, take that leap; beside you I will never leave." The bed the last to be moved, I pause, repeating, "Will never lose." I pick up the bed, and there as my assurance for me to see, your angel feather reminding me together we will always be. You are holding your promise to help me increase my ability in listening and in what I see. And now, I must do my part and trust, my leap of faith a must.

As I rode my bike on our trail today, I think of Ginger, who you have brought our way. I realized she is not only gaining home; she will be blessed with you as guardian above. The bluebird in flight across my path today, its message of happiness, of joy, that it is okay to embrace.

December 30, 2014

Here we are again, near our routine meeting time; though not yet four o'clock, perhaps even more fitting this night. In twelve hours, we pick up your sister where she stays. Soon, for her, new smells, new experiences, new people, a new place. New, the key word thirty-two plus hours before the world shouts "Happy 2015"—new memories, new adventures, new feelings, more beginnings.

In the wise words of your daddy—you know he has always been my grounding Earth angel that way—"It is not about us missing or trying to replace." He says that in moments when I feel guilt for my excitement that our house will have a four-legged family member again that isn't you; he reminds me that you are with us always, that you want this for us too.

I can still hear you tell me, "Mom, I know you will need time, but you and Dad have way too much love to give to hold it in tight." Your unconditional message was, "Take time, but don't stay alone for life." I know you are proud of how we are honoring the gifts from you we received. You taught us so much about true love, with a whole heart, without judgment, secureness, all that we need.

Your sister has been in a shelter. We don't know the exact memories she made; we anticipate they aren't positive her first year of life she faced. Abandoned, she was found by a kind stranger who gave her warmth, food, and no more loneliness at night—temporary until the time was exactly right. Two hearts searching for her; her heart too filled with hope as she awaited her turn.

You opened your daddy's and my hearts in ways we never knew possible until we had you, and now we will pay forward to your sister that she is worthy of love too. You helped me find my inner shift from "less than" to "more than" enough; and now a soul is entering our home who needs her faith found so she can be loved. That is one way I will live for you, giving what you gave me, my beautiful Roo.

She will have you as guardian angel and I know you will help me *hear*. On her behalf you will guide me to help her through her fears. Once I made the change in my mind that I was not betraying you, so happy I am that Ginger has your love as well to help her through. She will be loved by three souls, actually more when you count grandparents, aunts, uncles, cousins, friends.

And our house will become home, sweet complete home, again.

HOPE

December 30, 2014

Part 2

Again, "I see the moon, and the moon sees me," as I lay watching our new family member sleep. It was only a wink for a short time, long enough to whisper, "By your side."

"I am watching over her, Mom. I will keep her safe too; she knows she has found love with Daddy and you. I saw your tears, and I am grateful to know, they were filled with joy and new love. You are living as I wanted you to be, giving hope to another who was doubting their worth to receive.

"She likes my couch doesn't she, though the opposite end of where I would sleep. I liked how she hopped up on the cedar chest, now in front of the window where squirrel watching's the best. I will teach her not to chase after them quite like me. But, Mom, you know I can't have her completely ignore chasing them to a tree.

"I see she likes blankets, your third 'heater hog' in the family, just like Hans, just like me. Hans and I both saw the glint in her eye when the 'slumber party' bed was in the make; we both told her those are the best family 'dates.'

"I see she has already found Daddy's weakness for longing eyes; we told her scamming treats is easy as pie. My heart skipped in happiness for Daddy, too, when she watched out my window as he left and when he came home. I know he has missed the window prints of my nose.

"I whispered to her to sit and patiently wait, give Daddy time and she'd soon get his plate. She did good didn't she Mom not whining or drooling on his leg? But she will cinch it soon don't you think? She's got that 'can't resist' face.

"I see her lying next to you in the entry room where you and I did the same, our last time when I told you the time had came. I saw you pause as Daddy brought the mattress in, almost uncertain if you could sleep on it again. Mom, she is so lucky to have you there for her on her first night. Remember how I slept on your chest my first time? I know, Mom, but it is all right. Remember, as we talked, now you have two of us, both now at your side.

"That is why I shined the moon as you watched her nap, my whisper to your soul, I am holding your hand. As you lie there tonight, your heart expanding to let her in, let peace rest as well, for a new path begins. You and I will keep refining our new way we communicate, while we help a little one—my sister—find faith. She will be learning trust, that love lasts, that she is 'more than enough.' You and Daddy beside her on Earth and me above.

"'To the moon and back my love for you' is what you would always say to me; in the sky I came tonight so that you would rest assured, Mom, I will never leave.

"And to my little sis, Ginger, know I've got your back, and one more thing, you have a really great life ahead of you where you are now at. Take care of Mom and Daddy for me—they are my everything. And yes, they will probably be overprotective sometimes; it can be annoying you will find. Be patient and do what is natural because of who you are. Love them unconditionally for their greatest want is you never experience harm. They will always strive to love you as equally. And, Ginger, thank you for finding them; once again they are complete."

December 31, 2014

An annual tradition for the past few years, ceremonial in offering as a new year nears. Written on paper what is time to let go, patterns to change, pain to heal, the breaks of habits old. Written, too, are the goals, hopes, and dreams. Offering a prayer for what the year ahead will bring.

Outside in Nature, a candle, a matchstick to begin the flame, the paper containing the words positioned in place. Kneeling in humbleness for Universal love, with grace and in gratitude, watching the fire's smoke rise above.

History would have me conducting this ceremony alone; or with you not far, opting to scout and roam. Today was different, new, symbolic of where I have been and where I am traveling to. Independence, and hiding the spiritual part of me, replaced by courage to fully be. Your daddy, Ginger, and you all a part of the sacrament today, vulnerability and a willingness to be "seen" now in place.

Once outside, we found the location, a new spot to kneel this time, Daddy helping me counter the wind's gusty might. Slowly, then more vigorously, the words to ashes, as the flame's light grew, the Universe whispering, "We are listening, we have heard, we are here for you." I feel the Universe's warm embrace, it's assurance through you, keep the faith. Ginger and Daddy there beside me, going forward, new beginnings, family.

I have a dear friend who has stated so eloquently that when she frets, a thank-you doesn't capture her feelings sufficiently. "You know my heart," she will say; and no other words are needed, a *knowing* through feelings conveyed. I can't begin to express the powerfulness of what washed over me today, but since I know the Universe knows my heart, no need to explain.

Peace and hope wrapped tightly around my soul; grounded in family, faith, and love. Prepared to move from this year, now, no longer fearing if you can, if you would, will you still be around. I now stand sure in knowing you will be for the rest of my life, continually from you and the Universe the messages and signs. Feeling so very loved and ready now to receive, for the gift from you included finding the ability to love me. Trust in what I can't yet see, excitement for what will come to be.

Affirmation my heart is known, no words I need to speak; once again the message to reflect what I feel, signs from the visiting turkeys. "Thankful, abundant, blessed," across my path for me to see, affirmation to my soul, to hope, love, believe.

Toward darkness I run

I listen to tone and I watch eyes; I am learning how to act in "reading" these signs. It has only taken a few instances to fine-tune this communication skill, to gauge when to approach or retreat. The teaching moments shaping a strong—very strong—independence in me. Money thrown across the table when asking for a school need, enabling a vow within that on another I will not lean. If eyes do not sparkle, if they snap anger or disharmony, I know to hide or alter my behavior to fit what I perceive others need. If the voice I hear sounds frustrated or disapproving, I will find a safe haven to keep my heart close to me.

A fire in the night, the car no longer functional from an electrical system that's not right. Not the best birthday greeting but certainly it will still be okay. I am so excited for this afternoon and the Ice Capades. A gift my mom planned to celebrate a special way: the music, the skaters—oh, I am so very special today. I will not cry, I will not cry! We cannot go after all for there is no transportation to drive. Dad needs his truck for his Sunday routine; I am not more important, I cannot compete. The Conservation Club, his friends, camaraderie through alcohol and a good card game. Today is not different; disappointment comfortably the same. From this day forward, birthdays will be a day to make unimportant to mirror me; I will control any chance of disappointment by helping others believe. March 4 is a day with no special meaning.

January 2, 2015

Once again, I am shown how each moment connects to a future moment we cannot yet see, yet so purposeful for setting the stage of what is to be. Affirmation of why we should let go of the reins of control, the fears of change. Why we should trust, allow, pause, and step out of our own way.

As I drove home tonight with the sunroof open to see the moon, I reflected on a drive over a year ago when the sky was my view. I was en route at 1:00 a.m. beginning a four-hour drive, determined to reach my destination before starting time. A trail run I was looking forward to that I needed to complete, for in achievement I would seal the realization I was "enough" as me.

Days prior to the run, I experienced the ending of loyalty, of recognizing I had put others first at the sacrifice of who I should be. I was arm wrestling betrayal by three who had been talking about all that I was not when I had believed they valued me more. The conversation somersaulting through every inch of me focused on what had occurred among us four. In the replay, I was the younger self again proud of a grade and I was the younger self again feeling shame. Until I could see years later that he believed in me more than I believed in myself, each time Dad said, "Why is the B-plus not an A-minus?" unworthy is all I felt. "Please like me, please be proud of me, I will mold myself to what I think you want or need." My internal mantra that began to shape my approach to many a relationship—"I am enough if I believe your acceptance I've received."

I knew in completing this race I would find what I was now willing to stand up for regardless of price. Envious before of people who had a cause for which they were so strongly willing to fight. Like those who are willing, at all costs, I had found at long last, what I could not allow to get lost. Emerging as something worth fighting for, who I am I will not hide anymore. The actions of the three I could no longer blame, for it was actually a gift they had brought my way. No longer was I willing to lift others' pedestals by keeping myself at bay; respect needed to begin within before I could ask others to give theirs away.

As I drove this evening, I felt safety in the starlit night; each time I looked up, I knew all would be all right. Perhaps it was that evening then that integration with the stars began, long before you and I, baby girl, would walk in the dewy grass. I am still comforted by the stars above, feeling safe, feeling grounded, feeling loved. Sharing the four o'clock morning walks with you, solidifying peace when the night is in view.

I remember when Daddy mentioned moving the hope chest, relocating it to the dining room; I didn't want to move it, symbolizing the reality of not physically seeing you. I "gave in," letting resistance go, but only after wasted energy a while as I held on to "no." We put your blanket on top, and tears sprang; you would have liked to sit there watching the squirrels at play. Daddy reminded me not to regret, that you probably would not have liked the height to set.

Now *precious* Ginger—yes, and thank you, Roo for helping me find an affectionate expression I like to say; I couldn't call her "baby girl" but you know how I like to add to the "birth" name. Anyway, now Ginger has found comfort sitting on the chest watching the squirrels and birds, and I know you are smiling at the watchful "huntress" in her. I anticipate you talk with her while she sits there, and once again I see, a moment a few months ago set in motion right where we now should be.

You continue to ask the Universe to help provide signs, messages to remind me I am not alone, you, and love, by my side. The Hawk that flew when Daddy, Ginger, and I returned home from our first run then last night the Owl with its call as we ran a second time for fun. The mourning doves that serenaded us with peace and love this morning as we walked. And then the turkeys again calling, "We know your thankful heart." I would not receive the messages as well if it hadn't been for the moments in tune to sight and sound you taught me, purposeful in the foundation of finding the power to believe.

January 3, 2015

For one who loves words, I am falling in love with the moments where none need to be spoke, where the feeling is the voice of what the heart knows.

Words will always be my teacher, my hand to guide my growth; they will be the vehicle to deliver and receive the message of "enough." But because you have helped guide my heart to allow itself to more deeply feel, I am finding a new way to communicate, to trust what isn't verbal is still real.

It had been some time since the waves had overtaken me, and I had felt complete, when I would be in a moment with you, Nature, Daddy, home, and feel an incredible sense of peace. The wave of oneness, mind, body, spirit, my life, and the Universe, no thought beyond the moment where I stand; moved to tears, gratitude abundant, surrounded by love, in awe of my life at hand.

The waves have come back for new experiences in new ways, but still that familiar surge that where I need to be is in this exact second, this exact place. Felt this morning when walking around the yard with Ginger, the bike ride in the rain, and of course the Hawk that crossed my path along the trail today. Felt when Daddy asked, as he, Ginger, and I held down the sofa as you and we would do, "Are you happy?" "Yes, are you?" Our eyes communicated what no words could adequately describe; you were still with us, we missed the physical you, we needed Ginger, we were grateful you brought her into our lives.

You had whispered to me last night, when I didn't yet fully feel in tune to what Ginger's soul wanted to say, "Give it time, Mom, it has only been three days." You reminded me that our souls knew each other long before we learned how to increase our ability to speak; I needed to trust, take it slow, know that Ginger and I would, too, find that level of connectivity. You reminded me that it took you and me time to put words to what our hearts could hear and see, to what our eyes would say to each other, what our touches knew, that words were not our need.

Tonight, as Ginger and I ran back to where we had started from, I recognized in her an element of how my mind thinks when I run. Her focus and her excitement increasing at the thought of the finish line, she too found a renewed stamina with an end in sight. You had told me when we met Ginger that, in part, our purpose was to lead her to worthiness as you had led us; tonight, I saw in her eyes the watchful need as we ran to know she could trust. You led me through every step, every mile I learned to do; now I was to carry your baton and help guide Ginger through.

I also know you were happy to hear my burst of laughter resonate through the trees; Ginger creating in her hops, skips, and jumps, giggles from me. And once again your whisper, "Another way you two have found connection without a vocal language humans know; you are each listening to each other soul to soul."

January 8, 2015

It has been a big week, this first full one of a year brand new. Not because of a rigorous schedule, but for further learning to do. I close my eyes and reflect—had I been held from falling over an edge? Or, had I already stepped off as an arm pulled me up slow, making sure not to let go?

It wasn't despair, perhaps my vision of falling too extreme, but a challenge to walk in partnership with the trust I had come to believe. There are always opposites to what we can see, two sides of the same moments, our choice in what reality comes to be. "All things new" I look forward to this year to bring, and yet, I stumble in shaking old habits to allow possibility. Some see can't when others see only will, and some see hope while others see only the dark and still. You helped me to see I am "enough," and yet as I work on stretching my new wings, I find remnants of the "less than" feelings I need to finally release.

It began with the body warmth, the outstretched legs as if a hug; an arm in return as giver of a belly rub. Snuggled among blankets, the stillness before dawn had broken through; the mind translating the heart, "Baby girl, I love you." Then a pause, the reality ensuring I am fully awake, not you I am curled up with, once again my heart's mistake. It is Ginger, your little sis, and I love her too; by the way, I appreciate your whisper, "It is okay, Mom, both of us feel it from you."

I am still getting familiar with having two four-legged souls by my side, a new experience for one is angel of Earth and the other of the Sky. You have passed a baton to Ginger for her to be the teacher now physically with me, while you hold on to another baton that carries the promise you will never leave. Instead of relishing that I am beside both of you, I was still trying to grasp change, letting that "less than" old feeling start to seep through. Does Ginger know that my heart stepped away momentarily to be with you? And how do you feel that my heart flutters in happiness with Ginger too? Because that old pattern of "less than" clouds my view, I started to let it spill into each day in the things I do.

But true to your love, and how you rally the Universe too, messages provided to remind me "more than" and "be you," "you are safe" and "we are here to help you through." It was many moments that came along at the perfect time, to reestablish the foundation I have come to find.

It was lunch with a friend, the chance to share words of wisdom that might bring her peace, reflecting back to me what I have been learning I now am trying to teach. As I said words that resonated for her as true, I realized that my voice was saying them from a place where I knew them too.

It was the chance to overhear talking by someone whose life was nearing final days; the sunshine, the birds in the snow-filled trees, the incredible feeling of hope as I sat in place. Though I don't know for sure, I perceive a cure would not come to be, but it was hope in the form of compassion, that love is all one needs. I was taken back to my time with you and your last days, when you taught me how to communicate in new ways. When you taught me trust, and no need to fear, beauty abundant, despite grief standing near. To be with *now*, and rest assured all things always fall into place, cross each bridge only when I have to, keep the faith.

The reminder, "already enough," when someone dear shared with me the power of paying forward a simple act of love. It was a journal, with quotes about giving to others, and a message, "Because my life blessed with the gift of you, please pay forward in the deeds you do." The journal could be used how the recipient saw best, with the intent that even if one pay-it-forward gesture is still a strong ripple effect. Not anticipating that her pay it forward would be in an effort to heal grief, using it to write memories for two grandchildren to know their mom when they were ready. Just as I find beauty, hope, faith, and love in this experience with you, dear Roo, I find it powerful that a small token as a Christmas gift is being used as a similar tool. To capture the essence of a loved one, to reflect on the many gifts they gave, to find promise that there is not separation, still with us in new ways.

As I reflected on the journey this week to reestablish my base, I felt you gently pull me back to another place. It was the day before the cuddle with Ginger, before my heart felt you in my arms. It was when your daddy and I talked of you and Hans. When my heart unfolded so openly, so vulnerably, allowance of pains held inside, having lain dormant, in wait, for the right time. Talking, sharing, releasing, letting go; certain I had healed pains that had been buried long ago. But what takes many years to develop, or let fester and grow, may need a little more time to finally reconcile and no longer hold.

This past week was about purging remnants of what was holding down pieces of the soul, that once cleansed would bring the ability to forward go.

Perhaps it was the white lights or the lingering of Christmas in the air. Or perhaps it was my heart, reflecting contentment to the trees no longer bare. Just a blink in time before, the trees were not adorned in white, now through the darkness a blanket of peace, a soft, soothing light. The moment reflecting the quietness of my heart, a stillness ready for me now to do my part.

As I snowshoed under the starry skies, I reflected on last year's wintertime. I would snowshoe around the yard first so you didn't have to blaze your own way, the snow so deep I didn't want you exhausted or in muscle ache. True to you preferring to explore and discover the new, anyone following our trail would have often seen one track in circular swirls, the other straighter of the two.

As I snowshoed under the starry skies, in the window's shadow she watched and waited for me, your little sister making sure I was safe, and back to her I would soon be. In the night, wrapped in Nature where my heart most sings, I find myself held between the path I have made and the one to forge in front of me.

I stand still in trust that what I cannot yet see will be amazing, incredible, and full of all good things. I stand still knowing what I want this year to bring, learning how to say "no" so as to allow room for what I dream. I stand still giving myself permission to fully be me, recognizing self-love leads to selflessly. I stand still to recognize when a fear or old habit is trying to entice, and I need to counter with the certainty that "all things new" will be all right.

I rode my fat bike today, reflecting on why the hesitation about our upcoming vacation to Utah to off-road Jeep. I want to travel, and I think of my excitement for Greece, yet I can't seem to break into the same broad smile of this "out-West" possibility. Each pedal through the snow, meditation for my soul. And then true to one of the benefits you taught me, when exercising in Nature, answers received.

I am on the edge of change, I relish the thought, and yet— there is a tiny bit of fear of where I am being led. You taught me to trust, to hear, and see with such clarity; I am following what my heart whispers now, but it is still slightly scary. Your daddy has always been my grounding, so I look through a lens that keeps him in the same safe place, yet your daddy, too, is ready for change. He has always encouraged me to be, to make decisions based on what I want or need. He has not wanted my actions putting him ahead of me; don't be too independent, just walk beside him equally. Not always a strength of mine, but one I am learning.

You flash across my mind, the visuals that quiet within, refilling me with eagerness for how life may unfold. Filled with trust, with confident knowing, with faith in the up-ahead road. I have always envied your zest for life, your zig, your zag, that the world was as wide as you chose to make. I will honor you by meandering in the path I take.

Now I wrap up in the excitement of our upcoming trip and new beginnings, while enjoying the sureness of your daddy, Ginger, and me. The sun, the snow landscape, and there you are in flight, Hawk soaring toward me to my right. "On the right track," your wings outstretched to communicate, "Keep going, always with you, you will always be safe."

Now home, I run down the drive with Ginger, her eager hop, skip, and jump, her messages of trust and of play. She, too, has had to take a leap of faith. Bravely coming to a new home, her lightheartedness despite what may have been a harsh road. In gratitude for my life and this day, your daddy behind us as we make our way. At the bottom of the drive, in front of me in sudden flight, Hawk appearing: "Mom, once again, you have heard right. With you I am, go embrace the fun and the unknown of this wonderful life."

January 12, 2015

Is Ginger the one reaching out to be sure, or is it I grateful for the certainty of her? The picture would say Ginger the holdee, yet there is always more than what we think we see.

Before we felt ready to love again another four-legged babe, we would talk of how we would know it was time, what would be our gauge. When we would honor a new life for who he or she is, and not try to make them you who we missed. That we would be open to new experiences of what our third "child" would bring, then we would know it was time to share love, to move beyond our grief.

You and your brother are making me grin, loving insti-gators with your nudges "Ginger do this." Ginger's two older siblings influencing what she does; your communication, both of you still with us from above. When Ginger, new to a tennis ball, is teaching me to fetch from under furniture where it rolls, I know Hans is running excitedly, someone else in his footsteps who can repeatedly ask, "Throw, throw, throw!" When Ginger picks up a stick on our running trail, starting to dance in glee, I know it is your eyes sparkling, "Look at her, taking after me!"

And then there is your little sis, she is quite a smiler isn't she? And during our runs, yes, I burst out in laughter at how she raises her front feet. And, we agree, we think her knowing how to play is new, and oh my, it is good our floor plan makes for multiple round-and-round sprinting loops. And her dreams are quiet—no yodel or howl as you chased the squirrel—but a wag of her long tail letting us know she is a happy girl.

You know my heart, the healing I have been striving to do, to keep remembering your words and how best to honor you. In the wise words of your daddy yet again reminding, "It is not about missing Roo, it is about going forward to give more love," what you wanted us to do. Before we met Ginger, you had led me to reread what I had written as one of the essences of me. Always a dog at my side, for the duration of my life. And you asked me to look at the picture on my desk, a reminder of my encounter with someone homeless. A dog as his companion, to fill a need, yet there is always more than what we think we see. DOG equals GOD spelled another way, an Earth angel to guide his way.

Ginger, purpose to our lives, an Earth angel now by our side.

Entering into our lives to learn unconditional love, that she is worthy, that she is more than enough. Or is it that she will continue on your behalf to teach me? That in myself I need to continue to believe? Ginger is wise like you, in tune to our needs, at the heart level, the reassurance that she can bring. To bed with my more weighted-down heart, Ginger came to visit while I asleep. Curled up at my neck, cuddles without movement except our mutual heartbeats. Did she need me, or did she know I needed her? Perhaps both of us sent wishes for feeling more sure.

As we lay in the dark, snuggled close, in those moments, both saying through our souls, "I love you, thank you for helping to make me whole."

January 14, 2015

This morning you sent a message, "Mom, I am still with you,"
in the dark, in the distance, Owl called its comforting "hoot."
I am not sure I did my part today to wisely *see*, much more
energy spent questioning, doubting, fearing, not getting out of
the way of me. "Baby steps" is what your daddy says as Ginger
learns each day; these two words to myself I continue to say.

I am realizing the Universe is still needing to lead me back
for me to go forward in peace, that I need to express gratitude
to who I was for how she helped shape who I have come to be.
The person who did not believe she was "enough" needs to be
told she is loved. I recognize as I strive to release the pain, I am
sometimes caught in the exchange. The old from my left, the
new to my right, I in the middle trying to draw a distinct line.

I used to be afraid to go forward, afraid to change, and
now I am more afraid I will take steps backward, stay in the
"old" ways. I know it is taking a toll on your daddy—he doesn't
understand my distance, my mood, both of us caught in a fear
hindering us talking it through. I hope, too, you whispered to
Ginger that tears are not typical for me, that I will be okay, no
need for her worry. She was sweet to kiss my face, her comfort

intended to refocus my mind a different way.

The snowshoeing a good outlet, among the starry night and trees, reminders of you to help ground me. In the snow's light against the night, a deer bed indented just right. "Gentleness with self" if I could see the deer asleep, a reminder as I continue to run with grief.

January 16, 2015

I still remember when nineteen of them crossed my path, one of the first awakenings to animal messages that I had. Deer communicating gentleness, compassion, grace, love unconditionally; later, I would come to know it included not just toward others, but how I should take care of me.

Ginger's first experience, a deer to guide our way; I pondered, as I would when with you, what was the message it had to say? Tonight, the whisper was more than "gentleness," the prominent message I usually find; another gift of deer "determination" the communication this time.

The deer didn't immediately leave, standing in place for a few feet as our lead. Not an immediate dash off the trail when Ginger and I were seen, but a lingering and guidance to continue on the path to peace.

I felt it today, that change in the heart's beat, a shift, a tighter linkage somewhere deep. With you it was when I felt in my palm your heart at rest, promising you that your breathing would now be my breath. With Ginger, as she rested across my lap, her head on my arm; a sudden jolt, a new rhythm in my heart. Ginger and I connecting soul to soul, in the quietness of the moment, a wave of immense love I know.

This on the heels of clarity as I came to understand what had been gripping me. I haven't yet shared with your daddy the realization I now had words for; I will trust the Universe to provide timing for sharing at the right open door. Daddy already knows what I will say, perhaps not at the surface, but in a subconscious place. I loved you more than life itself; you were a child I couldn't bring into this world. Yet, you were my girl. In the trust you taught me, and in the vulnerability, I found a love for your daddy greater than the years of our marriage. For the first time I gave your daddy what he has always hoped for; no holding back portions of me with him wishing for more.

The hardest experience also the most beautiful time; among the gifts, letting go of fierce independence, bringing total self to role as wife.

As I gain strength in embracing the new, you continue to encourage my growth, messages from you. The Owl that talked as Ginger and I finished our run this night, the star that caught my eye through the window as I write. With gentle courage, I will forward go, carrying the beat of yours, my heart holds.

January 19, 2015

"Energy flows where attention goes." The quote crossed my path to read, summarizing well our Sunday together, Ginger, your daddy, and me.

It isn't the first time I have reorganized or purged the old; a closet, a drawer, a cupboard, moving forward and letting go. Saturday was another "house day," as I affectionately, happily, contentedly like to say. Tossing out, moving here to there, creating open space. Actions to allow new to enter and to take place.

Trusting I don't need to hold on to an object, how memory still remains; the heart always stamped and reminders you send—you are never far away. A rug you used to periodically rumple into a heap. I was always certain it was when your big brother was visiting when you tried to sleep. As your daddy said, as I decided the rug I no longer need, it is time for your little sis not to compete in her home with a dog she smells but can't physically see.

An old sleeping bag that saw many a slumber party with Hans—oh, how your brother loved our sleeping bag "dates." Serving trays that have never been used since your daddy and

I got them as gifts on our wedding day. A cabinet's contents reorganized so things were not stored cramped and stuffed together, no room to breathe; with each movement or release, I could feel lightness, a lifting, the shadow of new beginnings.

Sunday morning, Ginger and I cuddling, she stretched across my lap; no focus on a clock, no "have to do this" or "must do that." Making Daddy breakfast after he came in from outside, the laughter from my heart when his cold-weather hands touching my side. A run with Ginger, then the three of us going for a drive, more laughter as your daddy joked, joy resonating from deep inside. Couch lounging as we watched a movie, Ginger by your daddy's side; his smile, one that says so much through his watering eyes.

Another moment that whispered, "There is nothing else I need. I am in gratitude. I am complete." The words I wanted to share with your daddy, my "ah-ha" I came to know, played through my mind as it poured from my soul. "I finally gave you what you have wanted since 'I do'—all of me, no hiding portions from you. I became more frightened of going back than of stepping forward, another first for me. I can't wait for all of our new beginnings."

All of this said without saying it out loud to your daddy, yet I knew the Universe had passed it on for him to receive. In his comments, his tone, his eyes, "all things new" also on his mind.

Back to the trail, our family of three, Daddy starting out walking with Ginger and me. As we stepped onto the trail, a reflection of my feelings, turkey with its message "thankful" and abundant "blessings." Ginger with her leaps as we ran, running to and fro; back to Daddy, then forward again we would go. There in the distance, you called out to me, Owl hooting, "Mom, right here, you know I will never leave. It is okay you are purging the old, it was part of what we talked through; part of the lessons and gifts I was giving to you."

Sunday night came to a close with a movie you and the Universe wanted me to see, the last words of the movie so fitting. A message of hearing the whispers—we don't need the Universe to shout from above, and another of my mantras: hope, faith, and love. As Daddy, Ginger, and I lay in bed, Ginger and your daddy asleep, I could feel lightness, a lifting, the shadow of new beginnings.

This morning I shared with Daddy last week's fear, this week's faith, no longer hiding me; courageously I continue to choose forward, no longer do I need to stay unseen.

January 21, 2015

She gave me a gift that day she said, "Yes you do," when I admired her ability to meditate, certain it was not something I knew. Her wisdom reminded me it happens each time I run, when I feel centered, with the Universe as one. Her words resonate each time I feel the need, and again after, when I feel complete.

Today the power of being in *now*, in exercise outdoors the beauty of Nature found. Pondering how many may be too focused to see; do others overlook the blue of the sky or in summer the shades of green?

Do others feel the snow land on their cheeks as they look up through an umbrella of limbs from pine trees? Do they hear the stillness of an early morning before day awakes? Do they feel wrapped in love from something much greater as they stand in place?

Are they lucky enough to share these moments with a soul mate? Harmony heart-to-heart in every step they take. Baby girl, the giver of my sound and sight, leading me to a beginning in how I can better immerse with life. And now you are gently guiding me to notice what is directly in front of me;

another teacher is about to help you lead.

We haven't discussed the details of what our future holds, but just as it was with you and me, some things don't need discussion to still "know." I look into her eyes as she looks back at me, her whisper, "Trust this next chapter you are nearing, beside you I will be." After we met Ginger, the first night of sending assurances through space, "We are coming back for you, don't dismay." And that ah-ha realization of my upcoming age.

Turning fifty isn't "tomorrow," still a few years away, but given time is irrelevant, soon I will enter a next phase. Providing health doesn't turn in a direction that shortens the years of life, into early sixties, Ginger by our side. Where some might be saddened or fight the coming of a next age, with eagerness the future I embrace. I slow down my steps of rushing to the next, as I remember how many times "Not the destination, but the journey," you said. My heart expands in awe and gratitude, so many moments I am reminded of the power of the Universe and of you.

I am not sure if you were sending a sign to create a humorous memory we would fondly retell: "Remember that time we had to call the vet?" Or it was you wanting me to pause again tonight, like this morning when the day lay ahead. Daddy's call for Ginger's lemon drop escapade not the "Um, my puppy ate a piece of clothing; do I really have to say?" I know, yes, our experience with you I do laugh now; not sure too many others call for an eaten thong.

Ginger safe, no emergency, but as precaution a walk instead of our running routine. My heart swelling with love, once again your affirmation as guardian you will watch over us three. Beautiful Hawk perched so steadfast in the tree.

Have I noticed the rolling hill before? The backdrop of those trees? What a beautiful section of the woods, a first time my eyes see. Years on this path, the same lens looking at things, now looking around, new beginnings. The stillness of the water, my first look inhaling in a message of peace. A closer look, a mirror of surroundings, a footnote message, "Surrounded by love," much greater than me.

January 22, 2015

Slowly, step by step, though each one interrupts the steadiness of my breath. Tonight, it was changing a cover picture that has been my page since your physical death. It was our last "selfie" just before you, Daddy, and I took your last front seat ride. It has been over four months; I suppose it is time. I know you have been telling me it is okay to do. Did you like that the picture now is of the moon?

I continue to be humbled and in awe of your influence with the Universe and signs, that walking forward is not without you by my side. Your outstretched wings were the movement for us both, my body stopped in humble amazement as you spoke to my soul. Nearing the end of our driveway, you flew to me, so swift, so close, for a moment I feared you would hit the Jeep. I can still see the white and gray of your wing as you turned upward then over, your whisper to me. As Owl, "Ssshh-hhh, quiet now, continue to *see* as you are. You are loved, trust I am never far."

Just moments later, another message gently walking in front of me, "Compassion as purpose, you are surrounded by love, enjoy the journey, and *be*." I say journey and be, not specific to my deer friend crossing in front of me, but because the timing of you speaking to my heart was just what I needed to stop rushing too far. This week has been so powerful in you helping me to "stand still" in peace, my trust filling me with an excitement for all that will come to be. My foundation of *knowing* that what I *hear* from the depths of my soul is filling me with a joy and eagerness, faith in every inch of my being taking hold.

It has been the theme this week: "Not the destination, but the journey," "Quietly listen," and, "You are right where you are supposed to be." Affirmations and reinforcements translated from the whispers my soul hears are true, multiple ways you confirm "yes" and "be you." In an encounter or exchange of words with another, in the eyes of Ginger, in the animals you send to communicate what I need to know, all serve a purpose to continue allowing and letting go.

Today I reflect that my life can be divided into four thus far: Hans, you, Peppi, and Ginger each a significant part. I thought of you, Roo, and the chapter of my life you were a part; you were the one who helped me reach the center of me and an opened heart. You came just before the most momentous part of my transforming began; I anticipate you came just prior for us to build trust, so that I would allow you to take my hand.

Your brother Hans was with me the chapter before—when the start of marriage, a home owner, a job "in the real world" post college—the shift to grown-up was formed. Peppi was with me in my little girl and early teen days, when I felt most unsure, alone, "not enough," my most insecure phase.

Though there were dogs *there* in the chapter between, not a bond, not where I leaned. It was also during this chapter I was most searching, seeking, trying to understand. The furthest away from having faith in life's mystery, determined I did not need a helping hand. On the surface anyway, for in the depths I wished most for love to ease the pain. As I reflect on this particular chapter of my life without Dog, I am not surprised. This chapter titled, "Closed Heart, Shut Eyes."

Ginger now by my side, us building trust for the next chapter that lies ahead; I ponder, in a contented way, where I will be led. Another Earth guide to help me grow, to expand my heart in what it sees, to help me put the finishing touches on self-love so that I can be selfless for the world in need. It is often the opposite of what we think; I continue to learn self-love doesn't mean selfish.

I whispered to you as my heart overflowed, "I need a sign to confirm what I believe I am coming to know." Seconds later, your love I received, in flight wings outstretched as arms, you soaring as Hawk toward me.

January 24, 2015

I think your little sis felt you there like me, both of us looking into the trees. Every time I pass by, I search the branches and look into the sky. Though I don't always see Owl, I am certain you arrive there the same time I do, our souls traveling to a known rendezvous.

As our run began, once again I asked if you could show me gentle affirmations on this self-trust I seek. The awe I feel every time you and the Universe answer, humbled that I am that loved, grateful for the abundant support from above. A few moments after my heart sent the request, appearing a message from two. Vibrant red cardinals, one on one limb, a second one then into view, both whispering, "Self-confidence without ego in all you do, self-worth in a way that demonstrates living one's truth.

Surprise when your daddy greeted us running, Ginger and I, he toward us on my bike. I am not sure whose heart more joyfully skipped a beat; your little sis, Daddy, or me. Ginger's smiles, periodic head turns to make sure Daddy still is slightly behind but not far away and the feeling of completeness each of us felt, no words we needed to say. Daddy hands-on involved in this part of what your little sis and I do; I am reminded of one of my mantras this year: "All things new."

The stretching not physical, though that is also part of what takes place. Stretching as in continuing to learn how to reach beyond old habits and patterns, using experiences in new ways. When an old feeling stirs during a current conversation, more consciously I stay aware; I remind myself I no longer need to rely on the familiar—it is time to dare. I can change the thought or change the reaction. I can share out loud what I think and what I need. I can choose to be

Vulnerably, unconditionally me.

I close my eyes again to visually *see*, a way for me to quiet my mind by creating a pictorial scene. I am stepping back away from what is taking place. I am going to sit in the balcony and observe—as if for the first time something new I face. There is always a beginning when we didn't know: learning to walk, a first day on the job, traveling to a different country on our own. When the outcome's positive we celebrate, the memory of fear before we tried not as sharp and crisp. A far and distant recollection of being scared if confidence the found gift.

As I sit in this "seat," I will strive to greet each day from a place of excitement, with eagerness and a dose of laughter and self-forgiveness too. Not to discount knowledge and experiences but to remind myself past habits don't need to repeat in what I do. If something doesn't go perfectly, if I stumble, if sometimes an old pattern starts to lead, I will focus instead on the courage within me. An old pattern would say, "Not enough, need to change." Now, the pattern "more than enough" is taking shape. Growing to be the best I can be is now from a place that I am who others need; my best given will come back twentyfold to me.

January 26, 2015

Thank you for prodding me awake earlier then our regular meeting time, the most spectacular light in the night sky. There haven't been too many that we have missed, approximately 4:00 a.m., awake, most days since. Our time that we would go outside; I can still feel that comfort, loved by the stars up high. The view this time nearer 3:00 a.m. the stars blinking, each their own beacon to be seen, lighthouses as ports through the darkness, rays of beauty.

I anticipate you told the Universe I need continual reminders, messaging it once not enough. Your soul heard many a mantra I repeated in my mind, variations of "trust, trust, trust." Of course that was one of the plans you had for teaching me, one of our agreements for this life, your purpose, my receipt. By teaching me trust in our last Earth days, your hope that I would carry it forward in every step I take. I no longer repeat as many mantras when I run as I did with you; in the *now* of every step, trusting my body, trusting my spirit, trust greater in all I do.

The Universe yet again hearing my request, promptly responding to my need; the quote's theme "Patience and trust your journey." Affirmation again today in two requirements to turn left; much traffic making the effort hard-pressed. Letting go of hurry, breathing in peace—translation, embracing patience, trusting soon an opening. Embracing trust, certain in faith, another look left and right, safely the right space.

I believe those stars had another message for me: "Through opposites we learn who to be." One can look at the dark night, not realizing the stars need the dark to be the opposite—light. One needs fear to gain trust, one needs to feel less than to gain certainty in being enough.

The meaning in the words I know, but today this seemed to resonate deeper, applause from my soul. Some moments my heart starts to pull in an old memory, pattern, or habit, or I am caught in the spiral of "It is me to correct." I need to see when it is opposite either for what I am to learn or to teach, in that it will help me trust the life purpose for the people we meet. I had a moment where I felt I should still *hide* who I was for another to *see*, a twenty-five-year or forty-plus pattern that I have been working to release. "I won't be understood, liked, listened to," old habits still trying to interject; and then I heard you whisper, "Opposite."

If I worry the times I need to leave your little sis, separated, her feeling something amiss. It is not me failing her as Mom, causing her pain; it is the gift I can give her learning I will always come back, trust, her gain. Or if I wonder my ranking in her love, in the moments an old habit questioning, "Are you sure you are enough?" She hears my heart and a kiss or cuddle I receive, affirmation she teaches "Trust, believe."

Many moments to teach courageously "Be me, show up, stand out, stop the hiding." And then I will find the other truth that I know, what we give is a magnet for what we reap; positive energy begets positive energy. If I no longer hide, I will find opposite of the tricks of my mind. Another who I perceive wouldn't be ready to see me, will whisper, "Where have you been all this time? I have been waiting ever so patiently."

January 29, 2015

Your birthday in September, your brother Hans was October, both in the fall, your daddy's and my favorite season of all. The shelter that provided Ginger her interim home, their estimate her birthday for June, not exactly known. Perhaps because I had just talked of a race the weekend of your birthday or because your aunt's birthday is Saturday. Or maybe in one of those moments comparing Ginger versus you, or mine a few weeks from now coming into view.

Or, perhaps because you continue to help the Universe bring to me, opportunity to review for holding on to or leaving behind, replayed memories. I can still see Mom's car, burned, faulty wiring, waking up to the visual in the driveway; that single memory that put in motion stopping birthdays from being center stage. Reinforcement "not enough" because I couldn't get Dad to stay.

Do I have any childhood memory of celebrating my birthday with my dad? Or has it always been my mom making them matter, creating specialness anyway she can. Driving friends to a movie, slumber parties, a favorite home-cooked meal, a cake or pie for candles, making wishes always part of the deal.

Our wishes good but no match for the best she wishes for her children, those through marriage too; her happiness when she watches how each of our dreams comes true.

I think I already know my wish this year to be, that I spend my mom's remaining birthdays giving to her as she has given to me. And if I can add a second wish without greed, I would like to spend my remaining birthdays gracious in how I receive.

Often I listen to the deer as they talk with me, tonight their message additional in what they speak. Across the trail, quietly watching your little sis and I. Their communication "Compassion and gentleness," in front of us one after the other single file. Their eight whispers, "Remember, it is not just in your approach for others love and grace to give; yourself you cannot miss." Self-love, though not easy to do, is what allows us to fully let others' caring flow through.

I already have plans for how I will help honor you on your birthday: this fall our ultra trail run ten years after into this world you came. I will honor you on my birthday too; no longer trying to hide, but to let who I am shine through. An open heart to embrace celebration of the day I joined this life, thanks to you, Roo, angel of mine.

January 31, 2015

As I walk through history, I am walking past the barn-wood bookcases, into the green wallpapered living room—the carpet, the couch, the walls, the familiar feelings, all coming into view. Like a twin to myself as the child standing there, my eyes observing the imperfections everywhere. Wrapped in certainty, "not enough," I applied this to what was "just" a house. Had I ever felt its warmth as home? I cannot remember, greater the feeling of alone.

I have been "standing" in this room throughout the week, revisiting periodically the memory.

As Ginger and I carefully took each step with our feet, caution under the snow what we couldn't see. We knew below the surface there was more that might not be safe, but our desire to go forward leading our way. Ginger is like a metronome for the rhythmic movement of my legs, she leading as I follow her steady gate. Just as you would help me find clarity; your little sis, too, aids in the answers our runs bring.

In the trust you taught me to recognize the guises of fear: frustration, anger, impatience, emotions that can appear. These emotions also equipped with the capability to build an internal wall, to direct reason externally, certain it is what another is doing or not doing, after all. A few weeks ago when I feared going backward, frustration was the disguise, your daddy the receiver though he didn't know why.

If some emotions are a mask for fear until we take a closer view, then certainly there are disguises for "less than" and "not enough" too. As I look at each room of my childhood home, I am finding another word rising from my soul. A layer below my self-doubt of being "more," I realize I have not been seeing that shadow at my heart's door. As I run eagerly to the center of who I want to be, I need to stop running from "ashamed" hiding somewhere deep.

I have been sending gratitude to the younger me, her willingness to learn life's lessons to become who we are meant to be. I had been overlooking what else she felt as she sought to heal her pain, more than flaws to her she was trying to push away. Her home, her body, her closed heart, the rawness of "not enough," each sharing in their part.

Perhaps as you led me to the door of self-love, now Ginger's guardianship to fully embrace the whole of my life is enough. I have been aware of cycles to break, what meaning through the opposite of what we experienced, the purpose to take. I didn't realize that maybe some of those were prompting my heart to escape. A dear friend has talked about the "comfort in her own skin." I am discovering the key to this. When I can fully accept the crevices, ruts, and roughly worn road of my younger days, I will know self-love in the way that you gave. Unconditional, no matter the moment imperfectly, always your unending love for me.

Into a running routine

Certainly the loud crack means something isn't right, that I should be able to stay on the sidelines. Each time I kneel, the sound of the bend heard. Reason to be excused, though it doesn't hurt. A specialist to write the order that some gym activities don't have to include me. Now, I can fit in, though I won't be a sports star like they know how to be. But I won't be the slow one, the uncoordinated one, the pitiful sight to have to look at. They won't have to see how ugly I am, how fat. I can be the supportive friend who praises their every capability while I admire their skill, their confident beauty my envy.

It is thinning as I use it, tear-soaked. Oh, why did that have to happen? The sight so gross. The Kleenex no longer containing the snot from my blown nose, bursting at the folding and refolding as my hands try to find something to hold. I don't want to be crying—remember "Toughen up, buttercup." "Just go," my mind thinks. "I have had enough." He is leaving for good, divorce of Mom the next step. The assurance for all of us this will be best. I have wished this at different times in my life, but now the reality is validating feelings I must hide. I am not enough to make him want to stay. It is true after all, I am not worthy of *love or he wouldn't walk away. He is trying to assure me Dad he will always be, but his words are empty to my heart that doesn't believe.*

It was loaded with stuffed animals won at the fair and board games and I don't remember what else I took there. "There" not a donation center, or what would become our new home; there was a short distance I traveled in my mom's van down the road. Our field, a fire pit, memories I no longer need to keep; purging, the pain, a preparation to leave. If we have to move, these memories can stay. They didn't mean anything after all; from them I run away.

February 1 2015

From the right toward me, it almost seemed as if you picked up speed. You knew crossing my path was just what I would need, a reminder as guardian you always there for me. It had been a great day, and for a special night, I was on my way. You, as Hawk, affirmation that this process of letting go will bring reward greater than I can know.

This day a celebration of a gift I received, thirty-three years ago a sister for me.

Sisterhood, a bond, without limitations of space, hearts that can communicate without seeing each other face-to-face. When I see Ginger raise a paw in point or remind a squirrel to get back into a tree, I tell your daddy it is her big sis encouraging, "Like me, be." When my sister texts me at just the right time, I know, once again, she has seen into my soul and mind.

Common threads, yet differing, exchanges as student and teacher, each unique on the path life is leading. Your request for my attention was not in the form of a bark; your little sister demonstrates her happiness with a "voice" quite demanding and sharp. Middle night wake-ups common in you both, your methods to whisper, "Let's cuddle," a different approach. You would be vocal in your voice as you lay next to me; Ginger deciding it's time, a run down the hall followed by a dramatic leap.

My sister could teach the world to dance with her rhythm and grace; I can stay in sync movement with music, but leading the dance floor not my strength. A passion for new recipes, we both love to cook and bake; for me seasonings through recipes where she can tell seasoning just by taste. Though different styles we predominantly wear, we have been known to be dressed similarly when arriving somewhere. Planning and organizing part of who we both are, though her adeptness at grocery lists by store aisle is superior by far.

Both you and Ginger, each your own legacy vulnerabilities; testing, asking, "Do you still accept me?" We don't know the fears you brought into the lifetime you had with us; that we helped you heal and conquer them, we trust. We never abandoned you as we witnessed your concern, though we couldn't ease your mind that thunderstorms would never hurt. We don't know Ginger's life before our three paths merged as meant to be, but she too, has fears we are helping ease.

My sister and I, now more often floating downstream, our analogy for when we, with life, are at peace. Both of us have found home with amazing loves, continual assurance given we are more than enough. Both of us having grown significantly in our own self-belief, both of us still learning that honoring ourselves first is not selfish. Our fears are different in the how, the why, with certain dreams, or perhaps the same; unconditional love of self and others our mutual souls' aim.

Ginger is not you, nor are you your little sis, but your guardianship of her so visible I can't miss. I smile that though you never knew each other on Earth, your hearts still connected, you living through her. I have been blessed to know my sister since birth, our hearts connected, often our knowing without needed words. Our guardianship of each other, as sisters on Earth and soul to soul, pieces of each other's hearts to help make us whole.

February 5, 2015

"Chrisser world," your daddy will affectionately say, or perhaps sometimes his words come from a fearful place. I travel far, though I don't physically leave; your daddy recognizes I am not here, though still he sees me.

Sometimes it is an hour, sometimes a night, and sometimes when in process of another growth spurt, it is for a duration of time. Your daddy has always strived to give me the world; his unconditional love honors when my thought process is in swirl. He might ask what I think, and sometimes I may say; but he knows "Nothing. How about you?" is more often my response to keep him at bay. The inward reflection as I peel back the layers of me, how I best reach a deeper level to understand, to see.

Once again, I have been led to memories past, this one a summer job, an opportunity I had. Maine, a bed and breakfast, leaving the familiar, sight unseen. Ready, I thought, to take a leap. A change of heart, not leaving what I know; I try to remember what influenced my decision not to go. It wasn't love, but was it fear? That I couldn't succeed if what I knew was no longer near? A roommate, an apartment, opportunity to live on my own, yet still close enough to my value of being near home. Regret has never shadowed the fork in the road, my life complete. Revisiting this more about the "explorer" in me, experiencing the world through the eyes of new people I meet. I am eager student and something additional too; vulnerability easier with strangers than with those we are closest to.

Back in time, reliving camping trips—many childhood memories with grandparents doing this. My grandparents my safety zone that didn't require, nor encourage I abundantly speak. They aided in the establishment of "Chrisser world," my escape from where I didn't want to be. Home not always an anchor, more comfortable to leave; when feeling not enough, "elsewhere" filled a need.

Fear of not knowing what I wanted to "grow up to be," now in college so unsure of me. Maine was "elsewhere," surely "there" more safe; "here," as someone feeling "less than" hard to face. Not yet aware that the essence of me includes a balance of traveling the globe, offset with, at long last, relishing home. Maine was not for completing a missing puzzle piece of me; it was for running from who I was meant to be.

As I stand on the edge of an age shift, a feeling of "settling in" to me, in this "Chrisser world," I am reviewing my goals, my dreams. A dear friend calls it the "re's"—reassessing, revisiting, reconfirming, what do I want for me? I am starting to understand that self-love is ensuring it is, in turn, the best that others receive. I am finding the courage to share my wants as well as my perceived needs, requesting both are honored equally.

Dreams, wishes, goals, and wants are not without their fears. What if something I want doesn't align with those I hold dear? And then, you whisper in your powerful ways, "Mom, remember love, hope, faith." In your guardian image as Hawk, you soared above me on my drive, and you guided Ginger to be messenger tonight. Just as when you and I would run, and you would communicate exactly what I needed to know, tonight Ginger's reminder, "I will always lead you home." The trail uneven with snowmobile tracks, but Ginger's harmonic gait leading us nonstop to where Daddy is at.

I, in quiet mode, seek the atmosphere of my soul. My mind anything but silent, running rapid yet feeling slow. Along with trust, you taught me how to balance mind and spirit, practical and intuition, stillness to listen, and whispers to move and grow. I can still feel the moments when the wet grass a solid base, in the dark sky the stars grace in their radiant glow. The ground slippery, damp, yet held firmly by Earth below; the stars promise that the darkness doesn't remain, always a light carrying messages of "hope." "Chrisser world" helps me join you where you now are; sometimes missing the physical you is still a heavy weight to my heart.

The moon and back my love for you, your watch over me, and in the moon's light I see the robin's nest whispering, "Home you also need." And in time, I will return to the memories tucked deep, having let go, no longer their hold on me. And ever so slowly, steadily, without uncertainty, my voice strong, I will speak. The lines no longer blurred between run from and run to, all things exactly as they should be in what we choose.

February 6, 2015

So in tune to each other you and I became, I don't readily remember our beginning days. Certainly I knew together we were meant to be, yet not then aware of all you would come to teach me.

When you first came home, did I see, or more often than not did I miss how you looked at me? I hadn't yet started my heart's awakening, still keeping it sheltered, not ready to fully be seen. Could you see the fears I had not yet faced? Could you see the "not enough" I carried with each step I would take? Were you fine-tuning plans for how you would help me through? I am confident the purpose for our joined lives you already knew.

I am certain of Ginger as guardian, as teacher, a Universal plan that our lives entwine. I am still learning to hear her whispers, all the ways her soul speaks to mine. I know she whispers, "Being is far more important than doing. Chores can wait. Let's sit together before we start the rush of the day." And her joy when I come home speaks "Thank you for keeping your promise to me. Your return home helps me believe I am worthy."

There is a knowing in her eyes, a wisdom in which she holds the key; in time, she will reveal what she isn't yet ready to speak. She is watching, she too refining her plans for me. She will know better than myself all that I will need. Her gaze holds me close—I am held securely in place; and when our eyes meet, our hearts lock, neither of us wishing to look away. Our souls find comfort, familiarity, and peace; we haven't yet found all our words, but we each recognize the other is who we need.

Ginger, like you, is also in tune to her daddy across space, without a clock she knows the nearing of an end-of-work day. She also knows, as you did, when Daddy needs to be reminded that "more than enough" he is. Ginger gives the only thing she knows to give: her unconditional love, letting Daddy know just how much he was missed. She keeps reminders flowing throughout the night, cuddles and kisses as she lies by his side. And if together they fall asleep, I anticipate they meet up in each other's dreams.

As we turned down the road to home tonight, having completed our daily run, my heart arrested by the setting sun. The clouds woven together and outstretched, openings throughout for shades of red. A heart came to mind in what I could see, a mirror reflecting my own that beats. The openings in the clouds allowing the red's visibility, my heart shedding its covering. You have asked Ginger to walk beside me as guardian I can see, while you whisper, "Beside you always, all three of you, never will I leave."

February 7, 2015

I can still see her standing on one side, I on the other, in the middle of us the dishwasher on wheels. A gift—Christmas I think—meant to help in the work of making our meals. A cutting board on top, the resting place for my hands, the solidness to hold onto, in times I didn't understand. The kitchen the safety zone, her listening ear and unconditional love, in her presence, through her eyes, I was enough.

I can still see the yellow paint and paneling as I lay on the bed, and I can still feel the sorrow, the tears shed. Moved by the words, was it the story or my heart's release? So unaware then, eyes open and ears listening but not tuned into the power of these. I didn't yet know; messages arrive when we need support in our soul's growth. In what is spoken to us, in what we read, in a song on the radio, answers if we are open to receive. Perhaps *Where the Red Fern Grows* was a preview, the depth of love I would come to know. Or maybe the book a safe haven, somewhere to visit, escape, go. A book to talk with my soul when I struggled to speak. And Mom to catch my words when I could voice my fears and needs.

Fast-forward, just before I started leaning on you, another

passage with books and a sister helping me through. And then a dream. Its visual messaging. I was on the first step, about to take the spiral staircase winding and winding…down. Many steps, more than I could count. The bottom I couldn't see, but where I was standing no longer an option for me. It didn't feel courageous at the time; pain, feelings of "less than," walking "blind." Each step closer, drawing near, messengers to help guide the ability to let "more than enough" triumph over fear.

Then a pause in books as you whispered, "Follow me. I will teach you growth through what you hear and feel and see. In what we experience, in how we live. Together our own story we will begin. I will help you find a voice by helping you to open your heart; no need to explore through books, I promise you we will go far. Trust in the answers you will find, me your guardian alongside."

Now I stand with today, a circle coming around full, yet, curving in new ways. Each of us picked out three; books we will rotate as we finish each read. Replacing the newspaper that Mom would pass in routine; it had been our version of a book club each Sunday between her and me. And where once books were our outlet during our grief, now my sister and I reading for fun, not need.

Books now across my path intermittently, no longer the primary avenue for how I reach me. Messengers they will always be, but no longer an outlet for escape, a rescue I need. My soul longing more for connecting with others I will learn from and also teach; for interactions that are mutual, two-way streets. My mom and my sister, still guiding, listening, stronger than in my darkest days, a bond held together now through balanced give and take.

February 11, 2015

You were watching for us in stillness, with our guardian I
could see; you whispered, "I will wait for you," its regalness in
the tree. Your little sis was not hurried, so much she paused to
sniff, like you, scents not hers she won't dismiss. Like you, she
has a "zone"—momentary tuning outs of my call, "Let's go."

Once you saw we had made it safely to you, outstretched
wings and into the setting sun Hawk flew. Ginger and I continued on our way, our nightly routine to run at the end of a workday. As I reflected on your patience awaiting us to come into
view, I remembered the many times you pulled back: "Let's not
rush this through." The mantra you would hear my soul repeat
so frequently, "Not the destination, but the journey."

The parallel to life each time the words rang true, I was
faltering in patience, in trust, I knew. Impatient with my soul's
growth, wanting to reach *there* yesterday, not living my trust
that all moments happen exactly when they should take place.
And then your gift to me, an immense trust I gained, more
often "standing still," allowing, faith. As Ginger momentarily
paused on our run, I realized yet another way you are communicating from above. You passed on to your little sis to continue

guiding me: "Keep helping Mom embrace living patiently."

Ginger and I have also been honored with deer crossing our path; like you, they become her incentive she has to start running fast. I've always been wrapped in the comfort of their messages of compassion and love; more recently I have heard what else they speak of. Their encouragement to gracefully speak, with determination, yes, but also gently. Recognizing as I gain confidence in fully showing me, sometimes I feel awkward verbally. Like a child who gains a listening ear and wants to hold the attention tight, sometimes the words want to pour out before succinct in my mind.

As I blend trust of life with trust of me, I am learning the balance of blending in and being seen. A deer will be watchful and in tune to its surroundings, then gently take its steps. Across a path, if feeling safe, with a confident elegance. Nightly on our path, Ginger watches their trust not to flee; she internalizing what they are saying as part of her guardianship of me.

As I reflect tonight on you, dear Roo, my heart overflows in gratitude. How miraculous learning to better hear you, and now twofold growing with Ginger to also be in tune. As I write of your little sis, Ginger comes, curling up close, happiness her soul's communication she conveys the most. "Thank you, Mom for loving me; I will also bring you gifts you need." And with Ginger covering physical Earth, you communicate from above, through Owl who speaks, letting me know I still have your love. Once, when Ginger and I are outside, and then again when I look up and close my eyes. To the stars I smile, a wink from you, and a Universal prayer to hear one more "hoot." Seconds later, "Hello" through a hoot you say; my heart full, love, hope, faith.

February 12, 2015

You greeted me in the morning, wrapping me in peace, the brightness of the stars, and of course the moon my comforting. The start to my day a kind shadow each hour through, blanketed in happiness and love every step I would choose. Reflection on the drive home filled with gratitude and peace, in love with my life, loving the all of me. Revisited memories now replay without the urge to run away from what has taken place. Appreciation beginning to formulate a declaration, "This is who I am" and "It is now okay to look at me." And I smile at the younger version of myself as she stands still, now finding peace.

One reflection: a purchase to replace something old with something new; another shift going forward I choose. The purchase a want, not an emergency or need, abundance I have that I can buy when seeing. Taken back to only a fraction of what I know, as a child the sacrifices made for me in our financially strained home. Shopping twice a year for clothes—two seasons covered in fall and spring yet not understanding even that frequency did not come with ease.

A second reflection: a dear friend so wisely asked in a

profound statement kind of way, your brother Hans a reference she made. She asked if Daddy did? Or if my family? Years later, her words still resonating with me. "Does Pete care about the title with your name? Does Hans care the same?" Touching my heart, allowing it to penetrate deep, to internalize, shift, shed a layer of ego within me. I know it didn't matter in your eyes, my beautiful Roo. I as momma, running mate, Jeeping pal, a heart of love to the moon and back for you.

Mind. Check. Spirit. Check. Body honored too; harmony of soul, mind, and body as I redefine my relationship with food. With your encouragement that I could complete my first race, a shift in diet, foods eliminated, replaced. With each mile we trained for the upcoming "big day," a fruit or vegetable added, salty and sugary pushed away. My body never knew love, to become a vessel to appreciate and take care of. Each mile I run closer to my soul, the help to diminish moments emotional eating in control. With your teaching that I would increase what I see, now a slowing down to savor what I eat.

Written once when someone said, "Imagine looking back on your life. Write down what do you want to find." Excerpts from, but not complete; a glimpse to what I hope I see.

Where her light reaches, his light begins; where his light reaches, her light begins; there is no end to the mating of their souls, her husband, a biggest part of her feeling whole. Always soul connected with a dog by her side—her child in a fur coat, each her Earth guide. At eighty still running, strong and in a variety of races all across the world, still proving can and will. Her heart soaring at any form of exercise outside. Her writing, around the world touching thousands of lives. She always explored and sought creating in what she did each day. A quest for life learning, stretching past her comfort zones, seeking new ways. Her fearless sense of curiosity allowed her to see, travel, and experience places near and far; her unfolded heart taught others to see the stars in the dark. We affectionately called her Pollyanna; we are better for learning through her to see only the good, teaching us only that we can and would. We learned through her to hear and see, hope, trust, love, be. She wanted to add 472 people to her scrapbook—everyone across her path valued as a moment, season, or life; her scrapbook 472 one hundredfold she did find.

Looking ahead, to look back at what I would see, pieces of the essence of me.

Still more to learn, lifelong in the endeavor to grow, but closer, ever so close to center I know. Washed in gratitude and peace. Driving for home, your daddy and sis awaiting me. To my left above the pines, a large flock of thirty or more birds dancing in the sky. Certain you sent them to speak in at least two ways: "Ability to sway with the winds of change." And if not that, then perhaps this is right: "A carrier from the dark into the light." The exact message not as important as what was felt in my soul, surrounded by love, never alone.

February 15, 2015

Past the kitchen window in a blink, swooping turns, wings guiding in the blustery wind with ease. As Hawk you said, "Hello, Mom." You whispered, "Trust your day," and your flight pattern a message, "Come outside, you will be safe."

Like you, not held back by snow, always eager for time outdoors, any weather a time to go. Your little sis wears red, your coat was gray; her skin too sensitive to snowshoe, yet with a warm coat to run she is game.

"Baby steps," your daddy says of Ginger learning new things; something in common, Ginger and me. Out of her comfort zone yesterday as we went for a drive, a large part of her day not familiar despite by my side. Perhaps an element of her irregular sleep and her food schedule also nonroutine. All combined to her showing her fears in a negative way, misbehavior creating opportunity to wash blankets at the end of the day.

She sought reassurance that she still had our love, that in our eyes she was still enough. And in her snuggle against my chest, she was communicating, "I will help you too, Mom, through your test." Perhaps yesterday, sleep and food played a part on my fears too, causing me to keep portions of my heart from view. As I gain strength in hearing and seeing you still by my side, easier to revert to the comfort zone of old habits I find. Needs, wants, goals, dreams, certain ones still kept from being seen. When I freely share, when I show the full of me, my joy and happiness overflow from somewhere deep. Your daddy always so unconditional in his acceptance of me, whatever portion I let my guard down so that he may receive.

I could have said, "I would like" or "This is important to me." Instead, the moments caught in my outstretched hands push away the need. To ask or express, not my "typical" being historically; I love your daddy so, why shake his foundation of the "me" I perceive he sees? One small step at a time, "baby-like" each one I make, learning self-love is not selfish; we give more to others from this self-acceptance place.

Like Ginger, my negative fears came through, pushing your daddy away till a clearer picture was in view. Your daddy has dreams of expanded land or another house investment to make; and it draws closer this feeling I will be caged. I love my job, but I don't want it to feel as a "have to"; even deeper, I don't want to be as my mom, barely making do. It is a dream that my soul cannot shake—to write that others might find healing, purpose, and faith. A debt feels like a road that will wash away, no longer able to think and dream about "someday." Impatience my curse, stronger at the moment than what I know is true; all things happen as they are meant to.

This morning a brand new day, your gentle reminder in the moon "Make it matter, why I went away." You reminded me of your lessons on unconditional love and trust, that leaving my heart open to feel, share, hear and see is a must. In each moment when I whispered, "Help," there you were to say,

"Okay," as Hawk four times visiting today. As I came out into the field, snowshoeing as we used to do, there above the trees for me to view. My soul quieted, a visual that I need to further stand still and *be*, to not let external influences try to sway me. But I can't stand so still that I step back into the shadows to hide; I need to fully show up in the middle of external stimuli.

In the setting sun, feeling wrapped in love much bigger than me, across my path, another message seen. "With you always, keep going forward, I will help you through. And, Mom, so will Ginger, I sent her to you. Remember the feather I left you when you were preparing home for her to arrive, that all was well, always I by your side. It brought you peace, you were filled with gratitude, you trusted the future you couldn't see. Here is a feather for you, for reassurance, exactly as you are, show the world, *be*."

She looked back a couple of times, still seeking affirmation we are not far from her side. Your daddy watching me, without a word he knew what was replaying in memory.

Once again, I close my eyes, and I can see you running down the drive. Squirrels rapidly running up the trees, your bark, "Come back and play please." I knew you were once again coaching Ginger's gait as she too runs down the drive. "Oh, squirrel, I see you. You cannot hide." Thank you for your whisper, "Hi Mom, see, still with my family," a reminder beside us you will always be.

Not always in tune to their messages, but now I listen more. Squirrels encourage playfulness and their collection of sustenance to store. Perhaps because I felt I was the expert of how to pack away; not always aware of what they were trying to say. As I continue to release the old habits I've tucked away, there is a lightness entering my heart to take seriousness's place. I can hear it sounding different when your little sis invokes a laugh from me, the echo of uninhibited joy from somewhere deep.

My heartfelt words voiced out loud today, causing pause within, "Did I really just say?" I was sharing my readiness to show more of me, no longer trying to avoid, nor fear, being "seen." Outlining what I could offer, declaring that no longer external approval I seek, now that "more" I want to demonstrate is for only one person: me. I was letting go of the need for others to think "wow," "more than enough," "you are amazing"; stilled in that moment by awe and peace, perhaps self-pride, and certainly liberating.

A greater opening of my heart thanks to you, my confidence to show more of myself too. And now your little sis the guardian to keep my heart open wide, on our life voyage not stepping too far to the side. Ginger insists on holding her ground when a passerby comes toward us as we run, her soul saying, "I am as important as anyone." I am reflecting on the squirrel that didn't scamper away, you and I watching as it perched on the tire that day. Still slightly frightened, but bravely it stayed, I did listen as I thought it a message about storing up or making sure to embrace more play. Now, I think another gift was given in those moments eye to eye: courage passed on for me to apply. Perhaps also encouraged to begin storing for a change of seasons, a change I now embark; filling up with eagerness to fully show me and give abundantly of my heart.

Cheek to cheek, beside each other we lay, my heart listening for what her heart might say. Would I hear what she had not yet spoken or what I had yet to hear? More understanding of her guardianship of us, or maybe another of her fears. And then the clarity, her angst at separation not just for your daddy and me. She too knows motherhood and letting go, her story of what happened only she knows. Perhaps her void is even deeper, her breath gave others their first too; her understanding of the depth of my love for you, beautiful Roo.

Occasionally she talks as she dreams, like you when you would sleep. Her voice not your yodel or growl; we were certain was your joy at the chase of a critter on the prowl. Not fully aware yet what her dreams hold; may they be happy or healing the hardships her soul has known.

Does Ginger wake up from a dream and have its shadow stay with her day? Do some dreams contain messages to guide her on her way? Are some ever a premonition of what might come to be? I always thought I knew your dreams, until you helped teach there is more than what we initially see. Now I ponder if your dreams were a joyful chase, or perhaps sometimes they held guardian's direction, guiding steps to take.

I recount compelling dreams, those that embody messages for me. My most treasured, the one when you entered my dream, a premonition that in the future we would meet.

There is one that spoke of what my life would be: a clear message that I can still feel and see. Darkness, decaying trees, I was lost in the surrounding swamp, rising panic, fear gripping me. Finding my way to a building, falling to my knees, tears turned to sorrow-filled sobs, not where I wanted to be.

Like the dream before you entered our lives, resonating with the message of this one as well would take time. Grateful that my soul understood somewhere deep, a call to action within me. My life path was walking toward emptiness, a heart held so tightly for others not to see, the fear felt in that moment a gift, waking me to who I didn't want to be.

In the midst of searching to locate a centering of me, there was the spiral staircase in another dream. Each step circled around and down, the bottom step beckoning, though where it was I had not yet found. Walking each step with someone guiding my way, an angel along helping me feel safe. The stairway a symbol of the layers unfolding within, to examine, peel back, let go, then move forward again.

Other dreams guiding my way, and most recent the one lingering with me this day. As with the others, clarity will come over time, the purposeful messages I will come to find. Symbolism of the past, where we are, and the future ahead, and of cleaning the slate in preparation for next. Whispers of compassion, hope, and love, your daddy's wonderful heart, my life, myself, more than

Enough.

February 24, 2015

Do you laugh as I do when she sees her shadow come into view? Guarding herself against the reflection in the window her certainty she must do. Like you when disgruntled, Ginger's back ridged with standing hair, a way of communicating distrust of the moment, beware. Daddy or I will assure her all is well—it is the mirror of herself she sees; one more bark for good measure then your little sis is back at ease.

Your shadow never a concern, a mirror never your perceived enemy. Only your momma and her camera at times, your whisper, "Let's run, not take a selfie." Your surprise when I came home from that two-week trip to the UK, from a camera I did not seem to shy away. Home to you, I, no longer avoiding a camera snap; you, not certain where the momma you'd known was now at. Where did I learn to not hide from the camera's eye? Your gracious tolerance of each one capturing us side-by-side.

Your unconditional love drew out the best in me, that in my own mirror I would not shy from what I see. Each person we meet a reflection of who we want or don't want to be, who we wish we could become like—or fear becoming—in the traits we perceive. Reflection of who we are most like, where we find comfort in that, and where we resist and fight. The closer I reach comfort in vulnerability, the awareness hardest when looking into the mirrors nearest me.

A loved one who reminds me of my childhood insecurities, the self who struggled with weight is who I see. A stirring inside the little girl who viewed herself "fat," "ugly," "not enough." Who thought herself "unworthy of love." A little girl who perceived better not to be heard and not to be seen. Your daddy once again so wisely tells me—my worry about a loved one's heartaches she may go through, is perhaps my own history on which I'm imposing my view. Walking the balance beam, when to offer suggestions and when to accept "as is" unconditionally. The younger self whispers, "The pain is greater that I wasn't loved for being me." The older whispers, "Let go, keep your heart open, be willing to share if there arises a need." Doors open when the time is right; if I am meant to "help" I will know when it is time.

Another loved one who has always given me unconditional acceptance, no matter my fight to receive. Her heart always able to look beyond the moments in my place of insecurity. She holds the mirror to every year of my life, every step I take by my side. During the time I was furthest from who I was meant to be, the further away I pushed from her love of me. Easier to blame my weakness on what I was or wasn't taught, than to see it was her compassion and love I fought. Now I look into the mirror she holds, the one that resembles the goodness of all she is, and I find I continue to stand longer in front of it. She has been holding the mirror that she hoped I would look into, the one that says, "Love yourself as much as I love you."

Your daddy my closest mirror to view, the one I feel best

peeking into. The one I often miss in its reflection back to me, focused on my own mirror for familiarity in what I see. Carrying into now the collection of years I stared in the mirror of "less than." Testing your daddy, unintentionally but often, to ensure worthiness of his incredible love—I am.

I use the power of the Hawk you send in flight, recognition that there is always more than first sight. Often, I hear the mantra, "Not so different you from me," when I get out of my own way, so to speak. A lingering habit from the past will cloud what I hear, and later understanding that both of us hold the same fear. The how in our life learnings may be different but fundamentally the same, your daddy, too, healing his "not enough" pain. Your daddy has held a mirror patiently waiting for me to come to believe, what he has known all along in his love of me. At long last, I stand beside him not shying away, reminding him to look into the mirror himself, to see his worth the same.

Your little sis, our Ginger, is holding another mirror, peering into it as a start; her whisper, "Look, this is the joy of an open heart."

February 26, 2015

A faint whisper, or perhaps choice not to hear it louder than I do, your gentle words, my beautiful Roo. You celebrate how much more I live in the *now* of the moments at hand, how trust is getting stronger than the urge to preplan. And you treasure the recounting of so many of our wonderful memories, but you are starting to ask, "What about reflection on what lies ahead, on your wishes, wants, hopes, and dreams?" The anticipation, the excitement, the joy, the absolute contentment from down deep; that part of you is saying, "Mom, you also need."

"Mom, there is a part of you still afraid that forward looking means distance widened between you and me; you falter on what you know in that I will never leave. I always felt your energy at an idea, a desire, an ambition, the euphoric feeling that leaped from your soul; I still do, but more often I feel the energy of you reminiscing, holding on to your comfort zone.

"What about where you will be eight weeks from today, the experience in another country of a race? A half marathon in honor of me, a cruise around the islands, time with two dear friends, a week in Greece. Periodically let's talk about the potential, the planned, the eagerness at what might come to be; we can talk about the positive change these moments might bring. Greece, or the trip you, Daddy, and Ginger are taking with the Jeep. Or this fall and your ultramarathon race, in honor of my tenth birthday.

"I loved to 'hear' your thoughts as you prepared for a future event, your mantras and inner conversations willing your intent. Each run, each step, mile, and end point we reached, not only reminders of can, but symbolic of being one step closer to a goal or dream. The rhythm of life not just in the *now* and in learning from history, but also in pursuing, in the hopes you seek. The woodpecker that you and Ginger came upon laying at your feet, a part of its message perhaps time to add to the rhythmic sound of life's drumbeat.

"Our runs were the steady mantras like 'Can and will,' 'Mountains are only mirages so you have this hill.' Or 'I hand the Universe fear I release, back to me I am handed peace.' You have told Daddy that Ginger runs like your metronome, her harmonic evenness as she leads toward home. Among what you loved of me was my exploration of the 'world'—you felt I influenced your wings. My little sis, you sense, will be your grounding, she as home to return to after exploring. But Mom, as you say there is more than what we initially see, perhaps more learning for you and Ginger there will be. You, Daddy, and Ginger are about to go on an adventure to experience new things; the three of you looking forward, looking at

beginnings."

The sun's rainbow tonight on my drive, image of a pot of gold to find. And then a whisper, "Gold not needed, life already complete; what could be 'over there,' let's go see."

February 28, 2015

Today, a practice ride. One month from today will be our twenty-four-hour drive. Vacation, us three; adventure off-road, our Jeep. Michigan to Utah and back, your little sis with us every mile of the way, the longest road trip as a complete family we will have made.

We always struggled to leave you at home, but we knew your comfort zone. The weekend we did take you on a trip, your anxiousness nearly making you sick. We started to put aside going away, our homesickness if not with you every day.

I sometimes wonder if it will feel like my daydream, Moab and the mountain scenes. In my vision walking, mountains in the distance left of me, the sun setting; blue, purple, orange, yellow in the dusk coloring. I know I am walking toward a cliff, but I am not afraid; I hear and feel others cheering me on "this way."

Trust to be gained, to walk off the edge in faith. As your daddy and I embrace new beginnings, will Moab be the celebration of what you gave me? The daydream has not returned since I traveled with you to your new place; I now know my vision a premonition of what I was to face.

Every day since, my motivation to faithfully step, allow, *be*—each day's experience more incredible than the day before, you as my wings. Ginger's trust of us that she won't be led astray, certain I am that you guide her as you guide me every day.

As we enter the ramp that starts our turn for home, there you are reminding me of your love. Your white breast, your brown wings, some feathers atop your head fanned in the breeze. As Hawk, you remind me guided by you, your daddy, your little sis, the all of me, my beautiful Roo.

Quieter the echo of my heart as I run farther away

I am helpful, I am smart, I am the child "good girl," now to every-one the adult "nice." I have many friends, I strive to be liked. I am included, I am invited, I have fun frequently. But I am "not enough" to date, many times I am wheel number three. I don't have the looks; I am not one to turn a head or earn a second glance. I am comfortable not being noticed, yet sometimes I just want a chance. I continue to keep my feelings a secret so others aren't aware. Yes, many friends I have, but the all of me they don't have to know or care.

I have been raised exposed to traditional faith; I have been influenced by friends the same. I know well the feelings of guilt and of shame. These the pillars to keep me contained in being "such a good girl," so "very sweet." I don't seek spreading my wings should hell be my destiny. I am beginning to change now that college has opened a door. I am sobbing from such failure as I sit on Mom's kitchen floor. I am no longer "pure," and I am not married nor with a love of my life; further affirmation "not worthy," someone to love me I will now never find. Certain I will be judged, I embrace the familiarity of conditional love. I pack up my heart and I start the running game; I will find all of the ways I become the feeling I have best for myself—hate.

I am losing her, and I don't know what to do; she has always loved me no matter what but now I am a burden too. Why did he have to do what he did and take my confidant, my friend, my mom away? She has been through enough without his selfish act that day. Thankfully she wasn't the one to find him after he took his life; but now I am watching her struggling to fight. Her spirit crushed, she is searching to find her hold. I am scared... deeper within I will go. For too long now—years and years—I have watched her hide her hurting though she didn't know I could see; I am done with pain, I am done with feeling. Having an open heart is at too much of a price; it is time now that I close off mine.

March 6, 2015

Hello, dear Roo,

I love you.

There, now I feel you nearer to me. I can begin reflecting on what turning forty-six came to mean.

Now, also my tradition, thanks to a dear friend paying forward her family routine: "What have you learned in the last year?" she once began asking me. A question asked not as New Year's Eve is preparing to usher in the new, but a yearly routine when a birthday is bringing a year older into view.

I learned to enjoy cooking in new ways; a soft spot for my spice cupboard—hmm, what might be the seasonings of choice today? With each successful meal, drawn closer to staying home, no longer feeling the need to be on the go. I can still feel the enjoyment Daddy, you, and I had the Fourth of July; our first smoked ribs recipe we decided to try. Content as our family of three; cooking, relaxing, being together, embracing home, feeling complete.

I learned what it means to be a matron of honor, sharing this role with my sister's childhood best friend. Showers, bachelorette party, decorating, preparing for events. The goose bumps that said, "This is the one" to the wedding gowns array, our sisters slumber party the night before the wedding day. The walk down the aisle to pave the path to her dream come true, the wedding toast, my speech after "I do." My sister, an answered prayer when I longed for a sibling, an only child I no longer had to be. Her wedding the doorway, the catalyst for healing, both of us letting go our childhood "not enough" feelings.

I learned what it means to walk beside a best friend in her final days. To find incredible beauty, to feel indescribable love amidst the deepest pain. I learned to listen and look differently, to trust my inner voice whispering. The trust you taught me, my dear Roo, is carrying me forward in all that I do. No longer just words "all things exactly as they are meant to be" resonating such truth. I am right where I am supposed to be. At the center of me now a newfound certainty.

I learned when you let go of what you hoped you'd never have to do, you find incredible gifts, if you choose. A piece of my heart always kept safely right next to me, for no one else to get close to—that part I didn't think worthy of love to receive. You gave Daddy and me the most priceless gift though it broke our hearts in two; your daddy gained the all of me, no longer a portion I kept from his view.

With the gift to better hear, to see, to trust the inner voice that speaks to me, I learned an awareness of how I emotionally eat. Eating fast, eating though my body may say, "Not hungry right now." Though the food choices healthy overall, opportunity to change habits with awareness found. Recognition too, the power of sugar on my sense of hungry creating craving for additional food. Habits are changing as I let go of old patterns, old habits, as I reshift what my spirit sees in the mirror. As I learn to release any remaining fears. As "more than enough" winks back to my reflection and I fall in love with who I see, my body aligns to eating slow, listening to full, spiritual and physical in harmony.

My dear Roo, I feel there is so much more I learned, so much more I could write. And then you whisper, "Yes, Mom, but patience, let it unfold over time. More experiences await that will connect to what you've learned, what you are evolving through, and then it will be time to share them that it may help others too."

I stand in the woods where you and I snowshoed. I close my eyes. I see you running; I feel you by my side. I remember when you found it silly your mom hugging a tree; it was a joke for your Aunt J'fer, until I embraced the sturdiness held in my arms outreached. I stand at the base, I hear the breeze through the nearby oak leaves. They haven't yet fallen awaiting the buds of spring. In the wind I hear you whisper, "Remember that spot on the trail when the breeze would pick up speed, certain you were receiving angel kisses on your cheeks? Mom, here, a kiss for you, always I am with you, your beautiful Roo."

March 7, 2015

Twenty-two years and one day, and three days into forty-seven, time continues to tick away. I don't write that out of sadness or fear or any of the emotions heard in voices when people talk of fast-moving years. It is a before and after, an old and a new, a shift taking place as the whole of me comes into view.

This my first birthday where well-wishes are considered a bonus for any received; no longer seeking affirmation of "enough," to feel complete. Before, I would push away the celebration of me or feel let down when a birthday ended, that "not enough" hole still running deep. And as if a newlywed in my heart, our anniversary of twenty-two years feels like a new start. Our foundation built on amazing memories and unconditional love, your daddy an Earth angel to help me grow into being "more than enough." And now that I can give him what he has wanted since we met, the next sixty-sixty plus years our best yet. (Or maybe slightly less if the age of one- hundred and thirteen is not to be our destiny.)

Your little sis and I sit outside, the birds singing their gratitude for spring. I am trying, dear Roo, to stay in the current, to not drift back too far in reflecting. You continue to whisper,

"Apply what you've learned to what you now see. You don't need to keep recounting our history. I give you signs I am still among the living. I am not going away. We have talked of this more than once—going forward is okay. I am that tremble of excitement in Ginger at seeing a squirrel outside. I am right beside you and Ginger in the fresh air, in that sunshine. Talk about your laughter this morning, how you notice that's one of Ginger's gifts, and talk about how you are hearing her more, 'Namaste,' you said on the run today to my little sis.

"Talk about how you heard Ginger say to you, 'We are not so different you and I. I have chosen this life to learn *enough* too.' You know the moment, Mom, when Ginger scared you acting like me, when she ran up the driveway out of your sight: lost or hit your worry. She came back (I always did after I explored the world too), your voice and eyes communicated less than happy, not something she should more than once do. Later, after both of you stayed apart, you struck by her eyes, you saw into her heart. Internally she had cried as you also knew how to keep your tears hidden inside. She heard you say from her place where she already feels unworthy, where she doubts she should be loved 'I don't love you for who you are, you are not enough.' Mom, I know you didn't say that, nor did you feel it though your fears, but, you 'get it,' don't you, for how many times that is what you would hear.

"Talk about your love of Ginger as your shadow from room to room; her your companion in laundry, cleaning, getting dressed, her desire to be a part of what you do. Or about the runs that you and Ginger took last night and again today, your unified rhythm physically and in tune to what she had to say. Her pause not saying 'no,' nor stubbornness coming through; she is momentarily afraid, needing assurance from you. Your gentle touch rebuilds her belief, and in turn she is helping you train with pace setting for the fifty miles you will need. Or how in hearing Ginger, your own reflection you are starting to see, helping you be more aware in your moments of vulnerability.

"Or talk about the words for a friend that resonated back to you, in this life how what happens we choose. We first have to know hopelessness to know hope that we seek. We first have to feel unloved to then feel love unconditionally. We have to know fear to then know trust; it can be hard but experiencing the opposite to reach our goal a must.

"Or, Mom, talk about how signs are given to keep the faith, that those we love don't leave, beside every step we make. You know through the actions of Ginger in certain ways, or the Hawk you heard while you sat writing with me today. You know in the moon when you look up to the sky, and Mom, trust your feelings when you *know* I am by your side.

"I am in the now, I am in the future, I will never leave. Together we will help others know they too can heal their grief. We can help people find beauty in every day, and we can help people find assurance there is not distance, there is no space. Souls don't need words to still communicate."

March 9, 2015

The entire song not known by heart, just select parts. The words I say aloud or sometimes sing. Your reminders of hope and faith my request for you to bring. "I need a sign to let me know you're here," when I desire not just feeling, but also seeing you near. Just by saying that aloud, I feel peace; with a smile I add, "Calling all angels," then I wait, watch, soon I will see.

In the sun, white wings soaring majestically; my call, your answer, now crossing in front of me. Hawk appearing to remind me I am guided through every step I take, and when in need, you show you listen for requests I make.

My heartbeat raced, the way excitement grabs hold and the goose bumps say, "This!" a visual voice of the soul eager for world experiences. I read about Spain, Switzerland, Italy, France; the top ten or the fifteen best to plan. Or pictures of Washington or maybe a goal to tour across the fifty states. Or reminders of my bucket list: one on each continent, one meaning to run a race. Or if I am going to dream, visualize grand and without fear I would fail, what about a part of the Appalachian Trail? The quickening a reaction to Nature hikes one can take, speaking to the part of me that relishes exploring a new place.

In a few weeks, I will leave home without Ginger and your daddy, an amazing trip to Greece; and I know it will be the familiar torn feelings, excited to go, yet home I hate to leave. I will feel Ginger's heart, I will feel your daddy with me too, and yes, you will be with me as well, my dear Roo.

I am not sure which locket I will run the race with (the second continent of seven to run for my bucket list). I think it will be the etched owl that I have carried across two finish lines thus far; that one resonates most to what is yours—a very large part of my heart.

I enjoy the different foods, the culture, the sites from where I might be. What I enjoy most of all is the people I have the opportunity to meet. Each person an imprint, a mark left to mold me into a better me; my soul's scrapbook goal of four hundred and seventy-two pages times twentyfold, an opportunity to further complete.

I continue to refine the pioneer within me, to hone in on what about the world I seek. My spirit soars in Nature—to experience its scenery in a multitude of ways; there it is again, that rapid heartbeat wanting to plan every trip to take. But it is more than Nature beckoning; something much deeper within flutters my wings. I read a sentiment once about a puzzle, how we complete the puzzle of someone else as others complete the puzzle of who we are meant to be; traveling the world is to find the individual pieces that fit together to make me...

Me.

March 12, 2015

As I run today, in my vision I am at mile fifteen, with eleven more to go; I've been here before, this feeling not unknown. Or, actually, I am at mile thirty-nine, still eleven in front of me; it is a new experience—the same feeling to dig deep.

I have just let go of a life teacher (my dad), the best one I had for the first years of my life; to teach me the opposite of my purpose for this world, the goals I sought to realize. Or, I have just let go of a life teacher (you), the best one for near nine years beside me; you provided glimpses into each of the goals I desire to achieve. Not fierce independence but leaning on and with unconditional love. Compassion, self-worth that to my core sees I am enough.

When my father left Earth, it forced the breakage of the "old," the run from "not enough" to self-worth, a path I had to travel alone. Though you and your daddy were beside me, loving me every step I made, I had to find it within first to receive what you both were so unconditionally giving away. As I started to reach toward the center of me, you gently guided, encouraged, helped me believe. And when you knew I was ready, for you knew my soul, you guided me through to trust letting you go.

A gift I have been given and yet one that I can take to an opposite extreme, I listen well but sometimes hold within too quietly. I chose as part of my initial learnings not to be noticed, not to speak. Silent what I dreamed, felt, wished for, what I might need. And you, my beautiful girl, the perfect teacher too; for you enabled me to talk heart-to-heart with limited verbal words required by you. And now you are pushing me, "Take the next step, keep going, another teacher you haven't yet fully seen. Open your eyes, ears, and heart further to all that this teacher brings."

My independent tendencies to do it "my way" will sometimes cloud my view, and unfairly I forget just how much your daddy has put me first in all that he decides to do. Your daddy has stood at the sidelines; he has remained quiet instead of expressing "What about me?" He has hidden his fears, his encouragement for me to grow into knowing for myself what he already believes, I am

Worthy.

Your daddy's purpose to bring recognition to my soul, the one to show me the receiving, and giving, of unconditional love. Loving myself the first accomplishment, the marathon I didn't think I would ever do; now stretching to complete the ultra-fifty-mile run, learning self-love doesn't mean on my own too. The dream a message for me about patience, about not rushing until all things are in place, about fixing what is in front of us before anxiously hurrying—the act of running may be a parallel to living, but life is not a race.

Patience with myself not always my strength, easier to be patient with others when challenge they face. Calmness the energy I can bring to someone's angst, assurance for them to keep going, trust, in life and themselves have faith. My impatience not doubt, nor shaking belief; my perceived readiness when feeling confident, my timeline and the Universal plan sometimes out of sync. My wings start to beat as I feel the empowerment to soar, and I need to remember that is only part of what I am here for.

As you know well, for he was yours too, Daddy the grounding, the foundation, the one to keep us from venturing too long out of view. Your little sis my gift to remind me each mile I can reach, who will also always lead me home, she too my grounding. Ginger, too, the one my soul most comfortable when it wants to communicate, but it is time to give all pieces of it to the one who awaits. Though not easy after years of silently keeping it safe, I am not reaching the finish line of my goals if I don't start sharing what it has to say.

As your little sis and I ran back toward home, the fourth Hawk flew beside us in the same direction, affirming what I know. You as my guardian always by me, Ginger as my second guardian to home she will always lead. And your daddy is the half to complete the whole of me, *together*

Our life purposes we will achieve.

March 14, 2015

Her first ride in the Jeep today, not taking up as much of the front seat with her tinier frame. Yet her watchful eyes forward, running gear already clothed; once again my heart's skipped beat seeing an image of you when we would go. Today, I felt motherhood of two, Ginger beside me as well as you, dear Roo.

Ginger my helper, my shadow, my supervisor, and my reason to laugh along the way. As we spring cleaned winter's dust bunnies from baseboards and windows, I the recipient of many a kiss on my face. You might have watched me, but you were never my assistant from room to room. And if I started rearranging furniture, you preferred not to witness—not your comfort zone to have things moved. "Bound to have opposites when you have two": words I've said to parents when they share the differences in what their children do.

As Ginger started playing peek-a-boo with a blanket creating giggles in me, I pondered the times I thought you adorably silly. More immediate in mind, my remembrance of you as wise. I don't recall as swiftly your infancy when pup was your primary trait; I am sure you also had amusing antics that tickled my heart many a day. Or, maybe I wasn't yet as in tune to all you had to share, my heart still largely enclosed, unaware.

And yet, Ginger reflects similarities to you; I keep asking myself to check that it isn't my clouded view. She is her own soul, and compared she shouldn't be; my priority is honoring Ginger as Ginger and her purpose for me. I see her differences, and when I see commonality, I know it is you whispering to her, "Do this for Mommy." Today, I knew you were saying hello in the chipmunk that your little sis had seen. For one who hasn't yet discovered that squirrels run up trees, how quickly she chased after the chipmunk camouflaged as wintered leaves. In that dash to the chipmunk, I knew you were joining us on our run, and through Ginger you were having fun.

As we ran, my mind heard that same sound I have heard the last few days, a familiar alarm clock tone I couldn't initially place. Feeling a comfort at its sound, was it my two-week time in the UK when initial self-love I found? After your "hello" on the trail you guided another replay, and my heart recognized the time it was there to awake. It was our 4:00 a.m. times, your medicine and our walks under the starry sky—oh, dear Roo, thank you for staying by my side.

I know you orchestrate other angels to bring messages to me. All are eager to assist in what I may want, dream, need. Lately the messages, "It is okay to ask," "Believe you deserve that which you seek," and "Just as we answer immediately, trust that which takes more time we will also bring." As I ran in joy of my blessed life, I called to the angels for a sign. Running through the spot I have always referred to as "angel alley," the breeze like a kiss on the cheek. My heart whispered, "Like a mourning dove," being specific. Moments later, affirmation of the message's truth, the song of the mourning dove "coo coo coo."

As you saw and encouraged me to do, the couch replaced today, another step into the new. I felt your happiness for us, your satisfaction that I was still living your gift, as she and I sat together just BEing, not DOing, me and your little sis. As we sat on the new couch, her asleep across my lap, I reflected on the time you and I on another couch also sat. Continuing to look and listen just as you taught me, feeling Ginger, feeling you, my heart beating in peace.

March 19, 2015

There soaring high, a pair in flight. Dancing in celebration as I came back outside. I had just read to fourth graders stories of friendship, hearing Nature speak, of overcoming loneliness, of gained confidence, of bravery. A tiny arm in the air before I began, she awaiting the teacher to call on her raised hand. More powerful than she will ever realize in her words she had to say, "I like your blue dress," I was wearing today. Unlike the little girl I was when her age, her sweet words I could now gracefully embrace. Once a young girl who had never wanted to be seen, now the center of attention, eyes and ears on me. To the younger version of self I now gently hug; "At long last," I whisper, you can believe you are enough.

As I run, like an echo's last rebounding sound farthest away, I hear you, "Let go, let it unfold, the power of surprise yours to embrace." Then I hear, "The first step was to teach you to believe in yourself, then I taught you to trust that which you felt but couldn't see—trust even though it meant us together differently. You needed trust to open up to allowing, to not plan, to not try controlling what will be." And then your affirmation I have heard your message for me, Owl's hoot in nearby trees.

Your daddy tried once to join you and me on one of our runs; he on a bicycle to be a part of our fun. The summer biters—those deer flies did torment your ears so; the three of us forced to turn back instead of go. We would refer to Daddy as our best coach, for he would take us whenever we wanted to go, and patiently wait to eat supper until after we returned home. Such a supporter of our time together, you and me; but now as Daddy periodically joins Ginger and me, I wonder, did he ever feel left out desiring to be with us as three?

As your daddy bicycled beside Ginger and me, I found myself caught between the old and the new; my "routine" alone time now altered yet an enjoyment of your daddy being part of what I love to do. I am reminded again of vulnerability, how it can seem easier to be so with a stranger than with family. And I think of how at work change is relished, yet at home I like a semblance of routines. Why easier at work than in life? I look to that same little girl within for the awareness to find.

Work doesn't ask to be as close to the core of my heart; home, if I rely too much, could leave it broken apart. That little girl within whispers, "I understand acceptance of self, but still a part of me remembers the tears. It felt better to put protective walls of control up instead of keeping feelings near." I raise my arm in the air to the little girl in the mirror looking back to me, with questioning eyes: "Permission to speak?"

"Dear little self, I have found where you led me. Thank you for your unconditional love, your willingness to teach. No longer be afraid, no longer feel you are less than, no longer hide from the world to see. Thank you for your willingness to learn all that you did, to be you as you were supposed to be. Now, take my hand and together let's go realize our wants, dreams, needs. That is where you have been leading us, you as the courageous, beautiful, younger version of me."

Like our training to run, repeating each mile to rhythmic beat, you remind me again what you strived to teach. Dear Roo, that same view you and I took often, the trail ahead, the next stop we knew but could not see. Your message at the time, "Not the destination, but the journey." Now, your message that ahead I still don't know, but it is okay to be open to where the path may go. My heart is safe. I am right where I'm supposed to be; keep opening further, continue to lean.

Someone once told me I choose this life to learn two things: self-love and flexibility. Reflection on this day, the healing of a little girl within took place. Another layer of self now asking for new experiences, for the chance to learn and grow, to keep stretching, shedding, forward go.

March 22, 2015

Some might say, "That's funny," in an ironic way; for me
another demonstration of a miracle moment taking place. On
our way to our daily run, an errand incomplete, now food I
didn't want to leave in the Jeep. My mind thought, "Maybe I
will see the person along the way. I can give them this so it
doesn't go to waste." I sometimes forget that my thoughts also
cast a wish of what I want, need, or dream. And that I have you
and the Universe ready to help me achieve.

Minutes later, the person came into view. My awe and my
gratitude. This not the first time that I have been shown immediate response to what I seek, but each time it gets louder, the
voice I hear speak. "What do you want?" it asks of me. "We are
eager to give more for you to receive."

This time, my heart opens to embrace, the message that
requesting things I *want* is okay. And the awareness that's in
the quietness of my soul. It is easier to ask, to believe, to hope.
And yet something still holds back requests, still connected to
the old lens, the whispers, "Being selfish, just who do I think
I am?" Just as it was easier to share my dreams with you, my
Roo, most comfortable I am in asking the Universe to help too.

But the person on Earth who strives to give me the world in all that he does for me is the one I find hardest to share the depths of my dreams.

I am trying, dear Roo, to not step backward from what you taught me, to be comfortable with vulnerability. You helped me give Daddy, the all of my heart, no longer trying to protect pieces he could see. I am recognizing there are many layers to unfold in what that means, a tangible want vocalized easier than one that carries a feeling. If a felt emotion, then striving to control or analyze my tendency.

You began the lesson plans to teach me, the art of balancing, grounding with what is higher seen. Again, that wet grass on the bottom of my feet, firm standing in the *now* with you, being taught to accept what the future was about to bring. I wanted to have at least six more years with you, but stronger was your need, my beautiful Roo. I knew it wasn't for me to ask that you could stay on Earth with me. You had a far greater purpose to fulfill, your giving once again so unconditionally. You bring me back to this time when a gentle reminder I need, that I need to immerse into my feelings.

You have sent another Earth angel in the form of your little sis, her interjection when my mind is starting to run adrift. When my mind starts to turn and spin and find multiple angles to view, there is Ginger to redirect my focus for emotions to flow through. Laughter, joy, contentment, gratitude, courage to keep embracing the new. Overwhelming love, trust, eagerness for the unknown, unfolding in the belief of what I want to do.

All of these feelings coursing through me as your daddy, Ginger, and I walked the trail tonight. Days away from our family trip West, the distance, the location, with our four-legged child—all first times. My feet feeling the ground below, my eyes take in the sky above; surrounded by so many angels' love. As we drive home you appear to guide our path, your flight leading a few feet, then you perch to let us pass. As Hawk, you appear in celebration of my openness to continue to *see*, and to reassure that beside me always you will be.

March 29, 2015

I planned to watch you grow old, at least fifteen, or so. I didn't feel the same fear of yours as I have with mine; that I needed to maximize the years in your life. Your grandpa (my dad) passing away before he celebrated turning sixty made me think, in certain encounters, if I was no longer on Earth tomorrow what footprint would I leave. A force like you, one that I took for granted would be a steady base, taught me a great deal about embracing change.

As we drive through these mountains I am at peace, my heart resting in knowing all that is meant to will be. Now friends with time, its relativity, content in trusting what I can't yet see. Not harboring a fear I better hurry in what I achieve, assured time will bring me all that I need, want, dream. I will no longer worry that I may not double the age I now am, that I may not experience growing old; now faith life will be complete when the road comes to a close.

No longer holding on tight, and the newness of that sometimes takes me back to fright. Does it mean I no longer care? Is my heart slipping away? And then I witness the stronger bond when letting go of the reins. The more I replace "not enough" in my view, the closer to your daddy and little sis I am drawn to.

My soul stands on the peak; I am watching like you as Hawk in that tree. I now see the light I bring to Daddy's world—how I am "enough" to be what he and your little sis need. And, in turn, that I have taken for granted the depth of his love, a steady force for me. I have read the words more than once, "You must first love yourself before anyone else you can give it to." Now I am living this very wise truth.

At this mountaintop, my soul also stands in trust of the seasons as they change: melting snow to nourish spring, summer's gentle breeze, fall's colorful array. And the mountain steady, allowing what each will bring, evolving in formation, not worried what will come to be. If my soul was to start walking down one side, it would need to take each step one at a time. And so it is with my path to take it as it unfolds, trusting I will be guided in the directions to go.

As we drive through this mountainside, Ginger comforted in my arms, your daddy comforted by having near him his family. And you, my guardian Hawk, watching from the tree, with all three of us you will always be.

March 31, 2015

Perhaps they whisper, "Peace" or "Hope." Or something I haven't yet heard, those peaked caps of snow. They have spoken to me at each turn they come into view. Maybe they are speaking, "All things new."

It is worthy of a smile isn't it, how much your little sis is embracing this trip? No sign of fear in a new place not home, wherever is by our side her comfort zone. Your daddy and I wouldn't blame your little sis if she was scared another abandonment were her next step; so bravely, so openly, she trusts your daddy and me that her interests we look out for best. I can see your eyes shining happiness for your daddy and me, Ginger fostering encouragement to explore new things.

The mountains so majestic, so vast, so larger than life, their boldness spilling into the overwhelming love and contentment I feel inside. I remain in awe of the gifts you gave me, how through silence I found a voice to speak. How the purest form of love brings more to receive. How letting go of fear to be who we want to be shows us that we are more than enough for others to see. That I now have more credibility to help others also see; through the process of grief is the most incredible beauty.

I am in the backseat with your little sis while your daddy safely drives. Uphill, gentle curves, the brakes when the steep declines. The mountainous peaks, valleys, changing landscape, yet steady state. Standing tall through the test of time, weather, and external forces carving around its base. A shift, a slide, a weather-eroded fracture, or old falling away, yet constant, never disappearing, always solidly in place. Like the mountain, marriage to your daddy my steady state; no matter the external elements, the years solid on a majestic base.

Our anniversary now over—twenty-two years it's been; I can't help thinking what I would say differently if at the altar again. My heart at long last comfortable showing its all now; it feels like a renewal of my vows. If I in a wedding dress and your daddy my handsome groom, this the affirmation I would say with "I do." "In the words I say out loud in ways I hadn't before, in the words not said but the looks that speak so much more. In the way I no longer see you as opposite of me, my reaction, your action, intertwined from the same place, our degrees of worthy. In the open arms now ready to receive your precious unconditional love, I now give back to you a girl learning she is enough."

My baby girl, thank you for the feather along our family walk; as Ginger and I ran, the mourning dove's song. Maybe the snow-covered mountains speak of your light shining for us three, the sureness, steadiness, with us you will always be. I will continue to do my best to give to others what you taught me, to make it matter, your life's purpose, your legacy.

LOVE

The ability to run even when you can't see

My soul recognizes what my heart doesn't yet fully know, and I say, "Yes, and forever to have and hold." I feel special that day, the center of attention not too terribly scary. My husband's eyes when I come into sight give me permission to feel the meaning of beauty and caring. As Dad prepares to walk me down the aisle, I am still that eager child. My heart whispers, "Please be proud," the words are not spoken aloud. He does not welcome my husband to the family, smiles diminishing the longer I am wife; further away from him being proud of how I live life. A few weeks later his letter I receive. One word courses through the all of me, engraved on every inch of what I come to believe. I am selfish, and with that knowledge I further hide. And the running continues as I try to leave the pain behind.

Doing well in school followed by success with each job opportunity; I give my all in what I can do, for then I control what might be. I can define my worth by the work accomplished, I can feel accepted with each "good job" received. I can immerse into work so that I don't have to submerge into feelings; I can run from emotions that frighten me. I am seen, but I am invisible from view, a portion of me kept reserved while I strive to mold into what others want me to. Life is inserting change I can't seem to control; I am beginning to flounder; I am losing hold. I am testing the sureness that is my base; not once but twice my husband's voice, "I am scared you are walking away." I am living my life, but I am observing from afar. I am lost, and it is growing dark.

April 4, 2015

Before morning awakes, as evening prepares sleep, to the moon and back, your love guiding me. Shining bright after you nudged Ginger to wake me too, at our standing 4:00 a.m. rendezvous. And as our sunset drive neared the end, you gently appeared again. In the moments between, yet more lessons for me to glean.

You know my heart's elated when your daddy reads my mind, reminders of the power of souls joined. In the expanse of the mountains far and wide, my thoughts were a wish to stop planning time. The achievement felt when completing a plan doesn't compare to the awe felt in unexpected moments at hand. And yet still in such infancy of living this truth, more often striving to orchestrate then allowing the unfolding to come into view.

In that filled with promise, anchoring, I don't have to have it all figured out now kind of way, out of my mind your daddy's words say, "It can be hard for you and I to let things happen. We are so used to always planning our days. It doesn't take long out here [in these mountains] to let things happen as they will be, to pause, to wait and see." Though your daddy and I are similar in pushing ourselves to realize our dreams, your daddy has the ability in his words and tone to show our whole lives ahead to achieve. That I have awakened to spending more time standing still to allow what will be, is far better than never being aware of what letting go can bring.

Dear Roo, I am grateful that was one of your gifts to me; I can still feel the power as we lay in the grass with our only plans watching for the next cloud shape to see.

The horizon far and wide, and no wooziness of height. Was it recollection of my daydream that focused my view I was safe, or was it a gained trust through a taken leap of faith? On our sunset drive that familiar flop of the stomach took place, still with me those habits of the old, of falling down and away.

As it also is with my love as my heart expands in new ways, recognizing its behavior when it feels unsafe. It is new to allow such an unconditional wave of love to course through me, from that place of accepting self to embrace what I am given from Ginger and your daddy. When one thinks not enough to receive, love handed out unconditionally is taken in as conditional to fill the gap in self perceived. When one believes they are enough, it is the purest, truest form of love.

Discovering the center of who continues to foster that newfound fear not before known in me. Previously, in hiding that I was not enough for the world to see, now no longer wanting to hide, but still that concern: what will those already part of my world think? Are they ready to see the all of me? Or will their comfort zones prefer the mystery of who they couldn't see? And where am I willing to compromise, to change, or to stand strong as who I have now come to be? And as my heart stands vulnerable and open to your little sis and Daddy, I fear having to bravely, beautifully, unconditionally let go in love, like

We did, you and me.

We drive through the mountains in their purest state—no houses, nor electricity, no signs of civilization making residence in commercial ways. Always at the exact needed time, you appear in the sky as a reminder by my side. "Remember, Mom, to the moon and back, no space separates us, though the physical me now you cannot see. Trust, allow, keep listening and seeing. Let your heart embrace peace. Always with you I am and will always be."

April 5, 2015

Our first nights apart, soon it would be; returning again, the familiar excited to go, don't want to leave feelings. Your little sis had watched the unpacking from our family trip, and now periodically into the room she visits. I knew I had to hide the packing process from you, but perhaps with Ginger, she won't be concerned at what I am about to do.

It wasn't the suitcase, was it, that changed the look in your eyes? It was feeling my heart that would dim your twinkling sight. You knew my struggle to leave home and you, and your heart, wishing I could stay too. Was I seeing the same knowing in your little sis? Was she sensing her world soon would be temporarily amiss? Was she purposely turning her attention away? Was it sadness or her bravery for my sake?

My life, my being, such a sense of complete, not ready, if time could slow before I have to leave. I thought it easier to have spent seven days on vacation, maximum quality time as our family, the reality of separating harder than I planned it to be. I hear you whisper, "Remember what you know." Sometimes it takes me a few minutes to reground with my soul.

I know I come back a better person, for how through the

experience I grow. And trust in every moment is as it should be, and in Ginger's love—these things I also know. And something else, so true yet harder to face, another step in moving forward, that scares me I am walking away.

I celebrate the feeling of just how much I will miss your little sis. For I didn't think it possible to love again with the same intenseness. You always with me on every trip I made— my thoughts, the beat of my heart, that we were not separated by space. And you beside me still on every run, every step I take. I am now starting to bring along another running partner—is that okay?

Ginger into our lives I know your wish, purpose in all that she gives. Just as we loved Hans and could love you too, I know my heart big enough to make more room. I may not know parenthood in the sense of a two-legged person without a fur coat, but I know motherhood the same soul to soul. Slowly, and at times rapidly before I can blink, she is pulling me back into being "Momma" again, an extension of me.

Your daddy knowing what brings me peace, as well as an awakening of the new as his need. The evening before I must temporarily leave, your daddy's suggestion of a sun-setting walk on the trail for us three. Your flight into the trees as we began, then across our path as guardian Hawk, your assurance, "always can." My feet firmly feeling each step, grounded in the love by my side, your daddy, Ginger, you, all is and will be all right.

April 10, 2015

The sun's radiance shining into the window, just as with the moon you said, "Hello." Awaiting the train to begin the route to home. Was the gray sky that greeted me when I first arrived a reflection of my heart? After an amazing vacation, a sadness to be apart. Now the sun shines, the strength of your love wrapping me in peace; no matter the bumps that may arise to get home, believe.

In awe of the Belgium train station four levels high; trains to move people intercity, and others to travel through the countryside. These trains were taking people to work, to friends, to their families; the means to travel efficiently, economically, more freely. The faces in the windows tired but not afraid; relaxing or gearing up for the day as they make their way. I couldn't help stepping back in time to imagine a World War, cultural acceptance, and the overwhelming fear and hate; when people boarded a train not knowing their fate. What had it been like on a train car many years ago, when next was a prison or the end of life's road?

Reflecting on dinner earlier in the week, my honor of meeting gentlemen from France, Belgium, and Germany.

Learning of upcoming anniversary events spoken about as a "remembrance," generations later revisiting what had been. Hearing of countries once at war with one another now standing side-by-side, gone the barriers that fostered divide. Voicing aloud what struck me so, the healing that was now occurring from long ago.

In the moments at hand we may not always see the ripple effect or the circle that can come around to provide a different path to select. It is said what we are meant to learn comes back times over until we do, until we are ready to embrace the new. The gentleman from Belgium agreeing with my comment of healing, people ready to progress forward, his perceiving.

Was this trip internationally another circle for me? More choice in refining who I want to be? The city itself didn't spark an excitement in my soul, that desire to explore not taking hold. The people welcoming, warmth from each person met; gratitude for the opportunity to go, and yet. Perhaps it was practicing stillness to see and hear as you taught me; or my mind and heart still in Moab with my family.

I still feel the stirring to travel the world the duration of my life. A gentle tug to spend time seeing places I visit through others' eyes. But where I once was a sponge to every aspect of where I traveled to, I recognize I was searching for what I wanted to do. An element of "running from" was strong in me, and now I am eagerly "running to," excited for the future not yet clearly seen. Once, like you, I wouldn't hear what called to me, lost in my exploration, self-absorbed in my surroundings. Your passion to scout not greater than your love of home. Perhaps I could have trusted more each time you would go. Sometimes I called to you fearful you would lose your way; is this how your daddy felt at times when I left, though he didn't say? Now balanced in going, and returning, a mirror to the contentment felt through all of me; no longer searching for answers *out there*, my life complete.

April 12, 2015

The starting point many a time, gravel roads to get there on each drive. You would sit lazily in the front seat until our path turned to a gravel road, then alert to critters you might see steadily increasing your eagerness to go. Often I am thankful for the new trails I introduced you to, the best part of weekends that time with you.

The beginning for your little sis and me, expanding my accumulation of fond memories. Initially bringing her to where yours and my footprints had stamped remnants of our souls, seeking the places where you and I used to go.

Now this same mark the starting line to the race, thirty-three-and-a-half miles later the finish awaits. I reflect again on that race near two years ago, when my determination to complete it despite an unplanned hurdle trying to interject "no." Completing that race tied so close to no longer compromising me; running always that parallel to what life is trying to teach. Many fears were left in the woods that day. Carried out of the woods a new confidence in place.

Now, I prepare to run my first ultra along the trail where you taught me to first believe, from the initial step to the many miles you never let me doubt I would achieve. A time zone change from Europe to here will not be a hurdle to interfere; the all of me ready to be standing here. You awakened the *can* and *will* as the only paths I see, this race another fine-tuning of me.

My first steps, and I feel you with me. Now, mile one, the same location where we integrated with Owl—too many people today for its comfort to be seen. Mile one becomes two, five, nine; at needed moments a gentle encouragement on my path I find. The soft cooing, "I am loved," in song from mourning doves. And along my path the feather for me to see. Your whisper, "Keep going, I am with you, Mom. In you I believe."

At the halfway mark she eagerly greeted me; her tail wag and smile expressing, "In you, also I believe." Your little sis in that moment my biggest fan, her continuing the flame within that I "can." I know it isn't coincidence that Ginger is at the halfway point where the new is about to begin. It was rare to be on the trail with you beyond this.

We are a month past the halfway point of the first year of grief. Five months and one day from tomorrow from Earth you took your leave. Because you let me know often you are still with me, I am able to open my heart to the treasure we've received. And I know it is what you want for your daddy and me: Ginger our special angel sent to complete our family. I knew you were still alongside, even though the trails unfamiliar to you. Was it okay that I was drawing on Ginger's inspiration, too?

Now mile twenty-seven and it is completely brand new—I've known the distance but only up to twenty-six and point two. I've known grief before, but I have not known it in a state of grace; that in the greatest sorrow is opportunity for finding purpose, beauty, and in life an immense faith.

The finish within the allotted time for thirty-three point five; a comment from the greeter, "Look at that smile," when I crossed the line. The happiness fourfold, the contentment because of four too. Your daddy, Ginger, "I did it!" felt in self-satisfaction, and you, my beautiful Roo. I love you and always will—and you know the *will* in me doesn't waver when I believe; but I also know it is time, a new teacher is watching, waiting, ready, for more of me. Precious Ginger, your beautiful little sis; the next miles await with a new angel gift.

April 13, 2015

As I encourage Ginger to get water at the stream, I laugh in my mind remembering your first trail-side drink. I don't recall if your thirst was quenched, but remember my soaked running pants and shoe; after initial surprise our amusement, wiser next time what not to do. Perhaps because memory brought you closer to me, my accidental error calling your little sis "Roo" when a chipmunk was seen.

Tears at the rims of my eyes, what my heart feels, and hides. The lump being pushed down as it pushes back desire that tears be released, my mind trying to override the moment at hand, sadness and disappointment trying to lead. The sadness that I can't physically touch you, disappointment in self for disloyalty to your little sis too. You so graciously whisper your gladness to my soul, that Ginger is guiding us forward and through. Ginger, too, with all her heart gives to me; forgiving that I still hesitate, not quite ready to take what feels like a final leap.

My heart's pause when I capture her silhouette reflecting in the window pane, a perfect picture to greet using my phone each day. But, I can't bring myself to change, once again a wrestling with loyalty. It is just a screen saver on my phone, but it feels like you I am dishonoring. Your picture my first view, entering my password the opportunity to glimpse my beautiful Roo. Yet Ginger deserving to be a saved sight each day, many photos visible but more clicks away.

Tonight, we are three on the trail: Ginger, your daddy, and me. From the weekend my mind, spirit, and body aligned harmoniously. You know how a race always centers me; add that with the balance from cleaning home, cooking, and groceries. My joy, my gratitude, my excitement for how we keep experiencing the new, certainty we are living as you want us to. I know this completeness I feel is because of all I have experienced with you, and yet sometimes the wave strong in the void felt, how I still very much miss my Roo.

Always when I need it most, you come to me. As we drive home, there you are my guardian poised in the tree. A visit by Hawk with your whisper, "Momma, it is okay. Breathe. Peace. You know, you and me, together we will always be."

April 20, 2015

If given one word for your Hansey, "solid" comes to mind;
a rock, our steadfastness, a loyal base—all ways to describe.
What is one word I could use for you, my dear Roo? There is
"soulmate," "teacher," or "guardian"—any one of them would
do. And your little sis, our Ginger, a word that fits her best?
"Grace" whispers as the word that stands out among the rest.

True to what you helped teach me, in opposites we learn
there is more to see. On the surface, one would say Ginger has
a clumsiness trait, her excitement to greet sometimes cloud-
ing her judgment of an immovable object in her way. She may
bump into or slip and skid when your daddy or I the object of
her eye, but her movement as a soul gently takes life in stride.

As I knock on the door of another experience that will
certainly grow me, you as guardian orchestrating messages
I need. My trip to Greece in three more days, time shared
with dear friends, a destination run, island touring after
a half-marathon race. And yet there is a restlessness tugging at
a sense of peace. Moments when I am not ready from home to
leave. Your messages to gently flow with life, allow the unfolding in due time. You know my trust has grown, and I have faith

in what I can't yet see; but you also know my struggle with patience, sometimes discounting time's abundancy.

As your daddy, Ginger, and I go for an evening walk, your message of trust as my guardian Hawk. Recruiting support to reinforce, like your sis as my mirror for me, embrace the ebb and flow of life gracefully. From many a run you taught me to hear animals speak; your rally of them now to aid me. Turkeys across our path as Ginger and I ran, contentment with life their message at hand. The butterfly dancing at my cheek, reminders to honor the transformative process working within me. The deer that continues to show then quietly watch my passing by, its eyes communicating "gentleness with life."

Continuing to hear my weighted heartbeat; wings of flight across my path, I watch their lead. You heard me call out, "I need a sign," always ready to answer, to reinforce you're at my side. One messenger carried the message, "Glide with ease, let go of cares that try creating unnecessary worry." Another calling out, "Flow with the currents of life," and minutes later, another winged friend, "Soar over the stormy waves from up high."

I celebrate the shift I have made; of the future I am no longer afraid. You have taught me more than faith. I am shown continually my needs and wants are heard, how they continually take shape. Now, when I ponder what may come to be, angst is recognizing it is for me to request that which I would like to achieve, to believe I deserve and to trust I will receive. Confidence in self can be a little intimidating when new, unfamiliar, but oh so exhilarating too.

Greece will leave an imprint of which I won't be the same, but my self-agitation a broader reflection of how I might want my life to take shape. I will run the race in Athens in honor of you, and in tribute for the blessing of Ginger too. I will run gracefully as your little sis, bravely exploring with open arms like my Roo; and as self a blend of two incredible souls, my gifts of both Ginger and you.

April 24, 2015

You have trained your little sis well, my dear Roo, how in tune to my leaving home she is like you were too. Your whisper "Don't underestimate Ginger's wisdom—it is not just me. She, too, has the ability into your heart to see." And like us, but different, your little sis and I, are finding our own way to test, then solidify our connectivity that binds.

In the dark before the rising sun, Ginger's far and out of sight on her own run. Immediate fear, as I did with you. So uncertain of her return safely when not in my view. My fear acted out as discipline when she returned to me, followed by the ripping of our hearts as I affirmed home boundaries. Her devastation at her momma upset, my devastation our last hours before Greece had spatters of pain; not all moments of happiness on this our last day. The underlying thread, the foundation from which this moment stems. Can I trust in the process of life, or do I still interject impatience and fright?

True to Ginger, like her big sister would do, quickly her unconditional love given, so much like you, dear Roo. And yet, the run to unworthiness already my detoured path, picking up fear along the way so that trust didn't have a chance. You had taught me more than once "not enough" can cloud how we see and begets the opposite of what we want or need. Trust in Ginger coming back safely, trust in being gone from my family, trust in the amazing time I know awaits in Greece.

Now, starting the trip to Greece with road bumps, but once again the power of positivity. Intervening with another test, "Can I trust?" the message for me to heed. A flight delay when already conflicted, excitement to go at war with sadness to leave; a choice to make, through which lens to see. A choice to let go of the reins, to walk back to that part of me, to unite with the center that knows all is always as it should be.

Laughter and smiles the victor, faith wins; after a delay our trip begins. I feel your love as it reassures me, peace settling in with each leg of this journey. As we are driven to our first night's stay, an expansion within me taking place. My spirit's arms opening wide; is it the newness to embrace or your whisper, "More of my centering I am about to find." A friend's comment as your aid to speak to me, "Welcome home, kindred spirit," right where I am supposed to be.

April 26, 2015

The tears on the edge of cresting from my eyes to wash my face; as each step closer to completing the race. Your picture securely in my hand, the same one I used when prior I ran. On your birthday, and a month later too, just four weeks after you became my non-Earth angel, dear Roo. Can you believe we are here, a half marathon in Greece? Each mile a reflection of when you first helped me believe. From "I am not a runner" to many a medal I have now claimed. From "I am not enough" to telling the person in the mirror, "It is you I am learning to embrace."

Buoyed up by the voices cheering me, even though their language I am unable to speak. A smile, a clap, a "bravo," each I know, Universal certain communication encouraging "you can" and "go." The runner who passes, speaking English part of their skill, reminder that pace and form looks good as I conquer uphill. The volunteer who says in an accent with such melody, "Run strong. I see you again when you come back by me." Two miles to go, he is there again, reminding me can, will, believe. And, my dear Roo, once again that soft whisper that raises me highest of all. In the distance at the exact time needed, a dove's cooing call. "You are loved. Our bid to you peace." These the messages beautifully sung to me.

Another message you have for me; perhaps that part of the tears' reasoning. You are inserting a little more space between us, reminding me it will be okay; that I know you will never be far—you won't go away. "Mom, remember what you believe about dogs, how you wrote of one you met on a New York street. Remember what you are certain each represents, the description spelled backward—a dog the ultimate angel received. Dog reversed representing a Divine unconditional love, sent to walk beside so no life trail traveled alone. Mom, this dog on your run path today—another reminder it is time to fully see. You have been given another Universal soul, God's Earth angel to walk beside you on your life journey."

As I near the finish, my eyes open, and yet my soul a vision it brings. I am walking a gravel-lain road, you sitting as you watch me. Your coat glistening in the warm sunshine; such joy from your happiness with each step of mine. I am right where I am supposed to be; I can hear the drumbeat. A steady rhythm: thump, thump, perhaps the sound of ground to feet. But it is more—a soothing match of sounds; it is my heart in sync with your heart, my other half to wholeness found. Your brown eyes shine, cheering, "Just around the bend" the finish I will find.

From the left she enters, between you and I; your little sis—my Ginger—standing nearby. She patiently awaits, her hesitancy as she watches my eyes. Will I call to her as I walk by? My focus still fixed on you, her unconditional love giving me time to choose. I am not stopping, for the finish is calling to me; you are slightly farther away now, the gap between Ginger and me closing.

You whisper a soft reminder that comes clearly through—

your daddy's words again from you. "It is not about your love for me. It is about giving it to another who also needs."

You have arose, you are standing, you, too are awaiting my choice. Like the doves, your calming voice, "Mom, I am still a guardian. That will never change." And beside you soft green eyes, Ginger's face. Your words echoing in a continual repeat. I kneel down my hand outreached. Such softness, such warmth, my hand holds the most precious chin.

"Come on, Ginger," I whisper. It is time for you and me to begin.

I reach for my phone, one more step to take, a new picture as screen saver, to greet now is Ginger's face. The sun brighter as I continue on that gravel-lain road, all is well, onward I... onward, we go.

May 4, 2015

I am
home, and I am not the same.
Closer to self from traveling farther away.
I am a reflection of the butterfly dancing in front of me, "transformation" the message it brings. Ginger, my wise sage, watching her counterpart too; the second butterfly whispering to her, "Help your momma through."

I am comforted by your watchful eye, guardian Hawk as you soar upward into the sky. Your daddy, Ginger, and I on the couch in reunited bliss; quietly yet majestically your message, "You are honoring my wish." With arms open wider to precious Ginger so joyful to see me, affirmation in Hawk's flight, "It is right to let me walk farther away. Beside you, I will never leave."

I am a kaleidoscope turning in circles as I take shape, melding opposites into a consolidated picturesque array.

I am restless, and yet I am at peace. I am moved to tears in moments that touch me, some sparked by fear, other moments gratitude for love felt deep. I am uncertain, impatient, yet if I quietly be, I am trusting and knowing of the direction I move toward yet can't fully see.

I am becoming more afraid of there not being change, braver to seek the new though there is comfort in staying in place. I am healing inside, no longer the urge to hide, yet sometimes I still feel a little stay-behind-the-scenes shy. I am listening to the message, "Be gently determined, gracefully walk with life," and "Boldly believe in your dreams, can or will the only choice."

I am home,

and I am also in Greece.

Slowly, or perhaps rapidly, I am starting to see.

I am

Beautiful, worthy, amazing,

Me.

I am home,

and I am also in Greece.

In another lifetime, perhaps Greece was home to me. The language lyrical, poetic, beauty in how people choose to speak; perhaps my soul is finding it is home no longer in Greece.

Traveling with a friend who caught many a tear I don't usually release, matched with hers, both our hearts healing our griefs. Traveling with another dear friend also healing a severed heart, the three of us together finding purpose and new starts. In a country where language says so much, words were not needed for us to know. We found beauty, promise, and love in our ability to let go.

I am a kaleidoscope turning in circles, the colors taking shape. No longer searching for the one I've lost or perhaps never had in the first place. I am home.

And I am also in Greece.

I am returning to

Me.

May 10, 2015

Once again, I am comforted by you in the tree; your ability to appear when we are joyful as family. Your daddy, little sis, and I on our afternoon drive, you as Hawk perched with your watchful eyes. I heard you whisper, "This is exactly what I like to see—your bond strengthening. I feel your heart at peace." On this day of celebration, your daddy and I honoring the mothers who gave us life. I in gratitude for three souls that earned me motherhood rights.

Dear Hans, I have to ask, are you still spending time in companionship with my dad? I know, why ask a question I already know to be true; that lately both of you beside me as I spot each moral mushroom. Your dear Roo has been whispering it is okay to notice other angels that walk beside me, that I don't always have to focus on only her in my hearing. Fair enough, my Hansey, I can directly talk to him instead of through you. So, "Hello, Dad, I can see your grin, your glint in your eye, I feel your pride too. Your 'Kit' is successfully finding morals as you taught me how to do."

My Roo, I am still learning how you guide messages of what may come to be; more often my focus is on what I currently see. Three snakes as one encircled in the grass, watchful that your little sis would not notice and would continue past. Your awareness that I receive messages in Nature's living souls, that when they speak I hear what I am meant to know. You gently guided my attention to the three in harmony, together and then separate, their messages for me. "Our family unit," your daddy, Ginger, and I; that is what I first heard as I watched from nearby. Also I heard the whisper, "Mind, body, spirit aligned perfectly," as I felt a deep calming sense of peace. I also heard the echo, "Healing too," but since that has been ongoing, my listening to that message not as in tune.

The "shrooms" still her enjoyment, but the memories of *then* faded away; I the bridge between bittersweet history and new "todays." As I find each mushroom while embraced in Dad's pride of me, paid forward to Mom much love and her own healing. My purpose in part to break the cycle of a fragile closing heart, Dad in his own "not enough" pain; my mom, with her own life learning of "not enough" the same. As I stand close to the mirror telling the reflection, "I am falling in love with you," I feel the new circle coming into view. To my left is a shadow now in peace, celebrating my soul learned what he had hoped for me. To love without fear, I had to learn fear of love's pain; his sacrifice as teacher that I would gain. To my right, a shadow now in peace, celebrating her daughter's ability in herself to believe. Her pride twofold, also for herself too; "More than enough," Mom now whispers to her mirror's view.

I, encircled as one of three, you, dear Roo, and Ginger with me. To my left, you are the one who taught me to spread my wings, to step out of my comfort zone, to courageously stretch, to bravely seek. To keep going on the road to the center of me.

Ginger to my right, teaching me, stand still, allow, embrace home, stand firmly in self, trust who I am (becoming), external validation I do not need. You, on one end of this bridge I now walk, your little sis on the other holding her side firmly in place, both of you my anchors encouraging my leap of faith.

"Keep walking, keep trusting. Remember time is relative. You are exactly where you should be. Continue to have faith in that which you can't fully see."

May 15, 2015

I am beginning to, or I am ending, depending on the view, honoring your little sis for who she is, not trying to make her you. I am shifting from the wish your whisper she would hear. "You can do it, keep going without tiredness, the destination near."

Perhaps you, too, torn between your love for her and me, wanting to make me happy, but knowing better what I need. You as her coach, "Momma needs to do this on her own as part of her learning. Ginger, be who you are meant to be."

Ginger would run the distance if insistence from me, but her stamina better if our trail time more leisurely. I ran alone before, not every single run physically next to you; the longer distances when marathon training, the final days, afterward, when we couldn't be leashed together as two. But you were always my *pull*, my lead, my *fire* fueled by your eagerness to go, never an option for me to tell you, "No." Guilt my partner if I wanted to bicycle before you and I had completed our routine, you without a doubt my first priority.

Your little sis wants to walk, to take in the sights, smells, and moments when she can turn and smile at me. She likes it, too, when your daddy joins our walks as our unit three. I can feel your happiness that what you began has only grown deeper and strong, the new intimacy and comfortable vulnerability between your daddy and me we have found. You had led me to the edge of choice, doubt or trust, open up my heart or keep it protected and sheltered from love. With your strength I bravely stepped in the direction I needed to go. I chose hope.

Now, I run on my own, yet I do not run alone. You by my side, gently you whisper, "Listen, see." Nature's messengers you send to me. Just as you helped me learn the parallel to life in each mile together we ran, you continue to guide my trust that everything has a purpose, a plan. Just as you knew when my heart was restless, when I needed to befriend quiet's ability; you continue to remind, "Ssshhhhh, pause, listen, breathe, be."

The woodpecker who appears when I need to return to peace—"The rhythm of life," it speaks. The turtle I aid in moving off the trail that it won't meet a bicycle fate, at the right time it whispers, "Slow is okay, patience, you have time to wait." Or the snake whose message I can now embrace, "healing," no longer am I afraid. The turkey who reminds me my abundance plentiful; and the deer shortly thereafter to remind me with life, self, and others be gentle. And of course, there is the messenger you sent to walk beside me, your little sis, precious Ginger, grounded in home, in self, no external validation I need.

Ginger not meant to run in partnership with me; that I will continue to gain solidness in my own footing. Ginger the reminder of balance to keep: independence and dependence coexist now in who I want to be. Walking with family, running with self, increased time and miles in prep for September's race. Learning to gravitate to the new, to begin relishing unfolding change.

May 17, 2015

Last year, a robin with her fledgling. You were so drawn to that pine tree. Momma robin chattering so, when at long last your walk away, her relief. Of course, she became our messenger as we neared season's change. Late summer, early fall, many more years narrowing to only a few days. The power of motherhood she would remind us as she tended to her fledgling, her promise of faith in new beginnings.

This year, a cardinal and her precious little babe. Motherhood the symbolism, self-importance her visiting grace. Last year I, knocking on trust's door; this year, layers, more layers, trust deepening to the core. Increased ability to let go, widening the comfort zone in the need for less control. Experiencing the truth that love of self creates more love to give and to receive, the circle of reciprocation continually expanding. Faith in one's own ability to feel, hear, and see doesn't separate but acquires more received.

A balance beam widening as I let go of the fear to slip, more often eyes on the horizon above, not on the edge of abyss. Now the restlessness that can knock is rapping to the beat; "More afraid of not changing than of staying where comforting."

Before it was safer to hide; surely there was more acceptance if someone didn't know the imperfect me. Now, realizing others less accepting of what they couldn't see. "Not enough," I thought my secret, but furthest from the truth; what I showed was "less than" and "more than enough" kept from view.

The frequency multiplied, how often more rapidly losing count; your assistance my heart directly linked to Nature's sights and sounds. From our runs, you know how I came to believe, in the animals and trees' whispers I found faith in me. The floodgate open now, affirmations building brick by brick to solidly stand. Assurance in possibility, absolute in "I can."

I ride my bicycle escorted by butterflies dancing to the left, right, in front of me, *transformation* they celebrate in their messaging. Soaring high among the clouds nearer where I know you are watching me, the raven soars on the wind; "Rise above, look higher, there is more than what you initially see." I walk with Ginger, overcome with love; in the distance, the cooing love-filled melody of the mourning dove. Sometimes, you send guidance when I haven't yet sought it consciously; and other times you answer when I ask for assistance immediately.

I leave for work my same routine. To Ginger my same message: a wish and a promise to keep. A hug, a kiss and, "Someday I will work from home all five days. See you tonight. Always home to you, I promise. Momma loves you"—all this I say. Your precious little sis then awaits your daddy and I, her trust that in a few hours we'll return to her guardian sight.

Nearer the garage to begin the workday away, on my path a reminder I am not alone today. At my next step the feather gently speaks, "You are loved—surrounding you abundantly." My heart drawn to Ginger, my heart linked with you, my guardian angels leading me through. A second glance, a second feather, another layer of faith and trust. Loved and blessed I am, "more than enough."

May 22, 2015

Fragile is the layer that grows over the cracked heart, in one moment exposed to what had broken apart. Your little sis with signs her health needs to be checked. In an instant taken back to that first morning at the vet. It wasn't your daddy's first time seeking answers to what might be, but it was your momma's first sign to start listening differently.

Each step Ginger and I took retraced a step with you. Tests, waiting, and your conversations telling me I already knew. I was being tucked in covers lovingly by your daddy for you were now our angel with wings. We weren't able to transition your end-of-life passage by your favorite creek. I was sitting in the truck so desperately wanting to run back to the body no longer you. I was holding on to your last heartbeat in my palm, my dear soul mate Roo.

Looking at your little sis, her frequent turn to look at me, with her momma something amiss, tears not usually seen. Crying the reliving of our last week, crying the remnants of still lingering grief. Not fearful Ginger terribly ill, not from wavering faith; taken back in time, certain memories carrying pain. Replayed snapshots flash to mind, the circle bringing back opportunity a second time.

Choice to revisit that I might invite healing in, a freeing, a voice, "forward...begin." Another way to build trust in seeing life's beauty, that even when there is loss, there is goodness received. As you gently walk me through, you softly say, "Remember the love felt that day, though Daddy brokenhearted, his priority to be your strength." I may be on our trail with your little sis, yet partially my heart is in another place. As I remember that unconditional love, tears fade.

The same assistant the voice to help me let you go, now awaiting her voice again to let me know. From shore to sky through the cool morning mist, blue heron majestically takes flight, your morning gift. Its words "tranquility and peace," once again, at the right time, resonate for me. The test results negative, the special diet short-term, our Ginger's health a quick mend. And yet another way your little sis shows us the gift of why she was sent.

Ginger our healer, wise sage, taking us to new levels of unconditional love. Thank you for sending this precious soul, my precious Ginger, "more than enough."

May 23, 2015

Your encouragement to run four miles today, your certainty there would be clarity gained. You always knew each mile's rhythm had something to say, when your momma needed to peel another layer away. So close to the center, just a little bit more to go; a few more fears to push through, a final letting go.

The mantras are back with each step I take, the repeated declarations of can, will, trust, faith. Tuned in to the moments my body flowing with ease, listening to the moments when struggling. The leash around my waist more safety net than I knew, reliance on another to help lead me through.

You whisper, "What else? There is more. Closer, closer, reach closer to your core." Already aware of the fear "will I be able to run?" You and I would laugh each time I felt that one. After the first few steps you felt my heart lift—oh the rise. And you knew I was right where I should be, mind, body, spirit aligned. You also knew as my body toned, my "more than enough" increased. And I started to befriend the meaning of that word, "beauty." I had feared I would gain the weight that had stifled me. I would be that ugly young girl within, or how then I had believed.

So, yes, I know, we've revisited these layers time and again. In shaky moments, I need to remember to trust that I can. I need to remember beauty is when the soul is at peace, unconditional in its love. When it knows with never a doubt, it is perfectly imperfect "more than enough."

So new layers to unfold, what else has hold? I don't run like others, not like what I read or hear; perhaps I am fraudulent, that's sometimes my fear. What if others were to see the "truth," would they then laugh at or judge my capability? "Mom," you call to me, "it isn't about what others think. You know your body, you know what you can do. I'm reminding you again to trust you."

We continue to run mile three toward four, gently you encourage "more." Those who have known me as they have seen, what if they don't believe the realness of this "new" me? Maybe they will keep looking as if I'm still the "old." They won't believe I have grown. Those who have loved me through my unfolding, through discovery of who was waiting behind the scenes, will they be in awe or questioning? Hidden for so long, sometimes still in awe that this is me, with increased bravery the unveiling of my authenticity. What if who I now reveal isn't who they want me to be?

Am I strong enough not to doubt? Am I strong enough not to sway? Am I strong enough to no longer hide, to not shy away? Am I strong enough to no longer need external affirmation to define me? Created from within instead, I'm humbled by gratitude when compliments are received. Am I strong enough to stand tall on the purpose I am meant to live? To trust what I know I am meant to give? Am I strong enough to continue on this path of self-love? Have I built up enough foundation, from the very essence of me, to know I am

Enough?

Thank you, dear Roo, for the nudge today. You have always known the parallel I make. Portrayed into my run the life lesson I am student of; you knew if I was willing, the answer guide would come. The last of the base is being laid, the final touches near complete; it can only be done alone, an artist creating their masterpiece. Purpose achieved in every encounter when I wholly bring me. It cannot be realized if I bring who another has designed me to be. In the moment I didn't feel that leash tugging me forward, I still had you by my side. Strong enough, capable enough, with my own legs I am learning to glide. "This run on your own is the final wrapping of the package the world needs. Mom, you can do this, to the moon and back, our love. Believe, breathe, be."

Eyes as mirror to the soul, such youth yet such wisdom she knows. She didn't hear them, but felt with her heart; without my call, she entered into my encircling arms. It wasn't real, the story that carried reason to cry, only a movie, or perhaps it was more that brought her to my side. Was Ginger in my lap to dry tears for an ending of make believe? Or maybe she was in tune to other feelings.

Her experiences before rescuing your daddy and I, only she knows her beginning of life. She had been mother, signs remained. Not known how many or what of them became. Perhaps that is the wisdom reflected in her eyes, knowing the movement from heartbeats she carried inside. When she watches intently keeping me in view, maybe it is more she is understanding the times I miss you. When she follows me into a room, maybe it is her listening for her whispers too. Where her soul can hear no matter the space, the little souls wrapped in angel grace.

When her nose lingers over a scent perhaps it isn't to identify who else has been. I had always thought her trying to identify in her sniffs, just exactly who had tread on her perceived ownership. But maybe it is hope she smells for, the sweet fragrance she licked, nursed, loved before. When she so eagerly smiles, so softly cries. Perhaps I haven't given enough thought to the emptiness she feels inside. Her joy at both her mom and dad home, perhaps we are affirming she will not be alone, helping ease pain from knowing how to let go. When beside us, preciously sound asleep, is it of her first loves she dreams?

Into her eyes I look, as she looks into mine. Our souls stepping forward to further entwine. "I am trying," I whisper. "Just a little more time. Your big sis, she was a soul mate of mine. It is not that I love you less. You have quite thoroughly thieved my heart. You are not 'less than,' in my life—you are one of the best parts."

"I know you love me, and I know you miss Roo. I understand what it is to love and to lose. Mom, you know how you say there isn't space, that we can hear no matter the distance between. I heard your heart when it was reassuring me. We had met for that brief time when you and Daddy decided I could rescue you, then the three-day waiting period before the adoption went through. Mom, I heard your words as I slept the night we met. I heard each time they were said. 'Don't give up, Ginger. We will be back, I promise. We will be coming to bring you home.' I knew then how very much I was loved. I knew even then in your eyes I was 'more than enough.'

"Mom, we have both loved from the depths of our souls, and we have both learned trust in letting go. We know what it is to take a leap of faith, to reopen our hearts even when still so tender in pain. The laughter, the joy, the contentment we have found, we both know it is our purpose now. My little ones too young to be as wise as Roo, but they would want for us as she did too. We both know we are right where we are supposed to be, we each other's guardians on this life journey. We, too, are mates of the soul; found the day you whispered, 'Welcome home.'"

May 29, 2015

You are teaching your little sis another pastime you loved; she, too, checking the central air base for chipmunks. Like you at the corner of home outside, now Ginger searching for critters she might find. I am taken back in time yet again, another memory encircling me; this time the revisit joyful, not painful to see. I am beginning to learn the purpose in a circle that carries us back to replay; the chance to heal, so forward we embrace.

In procession I walk toward the stage, twenty-nine years ago, this same place. The red gowns, the white gowns, the family left and right. Can I remember what I felt that night? Days before I had thought I would feel a void; the night of "I can't wait!" joy. I am certain I felt older than I was, safe in that comfortable way, definitely unaware of what might await.

I walk confidently, no longer afraid to be seen. Board member now, no longer the student at eighteen. As each step is taken, I whisper to the girl within, "Back straight, head high, you have this." Healing has a wondrous way of entwining with memories, the then of who we were viewed through eyes and feelings of who we now see. I don't remember how hard that walk in front of everyone who might see. I don't remember the fear that gripped the core of me.

The class president speaks of purpose, of exploration, of the future's mystery. So eager to begin the next chapter of her life journey. I think I had felt an excitement too, buoyed by the certainty of my youth. I didn't know at the time I wasn't graduating on my own two feet; friendships, one or two teachers, grades I could achieve all while holding my identity. I had given a large piece of me away; only later did I realize it was a heavy weight. Reliance on others to provide feelings of "enough" before self-believed, shortchanges the others in what they could receive.

As the circle brings me back to then, in the now of me I've found, I am learning healing isn't doing over moments that come back around. It's seeing with new eyes from a place of gratitude. Who I am because of the girl in me I knew. The courage to locate my center because of the gift of you, dear Roo.

I now stand in the circle of celebration, the giver of "congrats," not the one to receive. Until once again I was shown the power of moments we can't foresee.

I did not know the person who had something to speak, her kind eyes and smile just before her impact on me. Gently touching my arm, she proceeded to say, "I need to tell you, you are beautiful." If only she knew the wave of healing she had just brought my way. In a scramble to find words that could adequately express my heart, the best I could do was whisper, "Aww, thank you so much," as I wrapped her in my arms. She continued to humble my soul as she spoke, "I always make it a point to give a compliment when deserved." So much more I wish I could express back, my honor of the gift of her.

I am no longer that girl who was "less than," but so thankful that she was me. Her pain I now release. No longer the urge to hide from what she experienced, no longer afraid of her feelings of "unworthy." Forward in peace, into memory—she is of courage and beauty.

May 30, 2015

"I know you need this time, I will patiently wait," words your little sis whispered as I started to walk away. Double meaning her soul communicates in what she says to me, not just the immediate run I head to, but also for the continued release.

This time they reached past where they have stopped before, beyond the surface, over the brim, held in no more. At the end of the run, tears the release—a blend of joy, gratitude, love, and grief.

You brought the mantra to the run today, two words from a song in continual play. "True Colors" humming in the distance of my mind; with each mile (of life) I run, closer to what I will find. The hummingbird at the window this morning reflecting my heart's greeting to the day; "joy" it's message as it flew away. Joyfulness and gratitude from last night's shifting; inward the letting go of more "old" lingering. Love overflowing for all the blessings in my life, for this walk with Ginger, our shared time. And I cannot hide the longing too, perhaps it is the trees along the trail recounting each run with you.

Through tears you bring a visual, a polishing, like a diamond or a rock, rubbed until its brilliant sheen. I hear you whispering, "A diamond in the rough, near ready for display. Keep going, Mom, keep peeling layers away." I also hear your caution no need to rub raw something focused on too long; acceptance just as radiant as believing healed equals gone. When one can look with laughter and thankfulness at what once caused pain, the gentleness of grace no longer requires *then* be erased.

More often than not my heart wrapped in sweet embrace, smiling at signs you are not far away. Knowing the void felt isn't meant to completely leave, I find comfort always, with me you will be. The tears another brick building the foundation of me, sturdier, more unshakeable, greater trust to be.

Now home beckons to me, Ginger awaiting her momma to greet. She is our precious gift isn't she, my dear Roo; Ginger our mutual messenger, letting abundant love flow through. Her open heart the pathway for you to speak, her unconditional love completing us as family.

June 1, 2015

In another place not where I am sitting as your daddy drives, observing the hearts of certain friends in my mind. They have experienced too being with one loved in the final hours and days, only they can know exactly their heart's walk with pain. Only they know what they feel, what their grief is leading them through. But the decision to honor a quality of life I understand too. They bravely walked alongside hope and faith, then let go to honor their loved one in their decision made.

I am back in time, farther back than you, I am stepping into and out of a hospital room. I am holding a cold hand before possibility would shrink, machines his sustenance—not how he wanted to be. His final breathing as I whisper permission to leave, shortly thereafter his heart's release. Our last touch, the warmth of his hand communicating to me, "I am happy, I am now at peace."

I look out the window sending positive energy, that friends can find serenity. Because you taught me such profound trust, affirmations that you will never leave, I know friends will be okay though at this moment that knowing they may not see. As my mind reflects on that weekend seven years ago, my heart can revisit the memories without sorrow's hold. There is a wisdom now in place that it is never good-bye; it is the ability to see someone in other ways, still by our side.

You are in the sky soaring majestically, your outstretched guiding wings. Your whisper, "I am here. You are safe. Continue to look beyond what you initially see. Continue to hold strong to your sense of purpose in all moments and all things. Your course through grief will inspire others to believe. All is well. Peace."

A gentle touch, as if a hand now rested on my shoulder in a reassuring embrace. Back into the *now*, a glance for who was responsible for the gesture made. Not your daddy; this loving touch felt directly behind me. Your precious little sis the one to know what I would need, to "pull me" back into the moment so I wouldn't dwell on my historical memories.

Loss individualized, each person with their own breakage. Steps toward hope, faith, gratitude, goodness from sorrow if receptive to see. Sometimes words cannot ease the pain; sometimes words aren't needed to help explain. In the moments when so loudly the felt void screams, the greatest opportunity to hear our loved one speak. In what our eyes observe, in Nature's sounds, in our heart's flutter the messages abound.

May time softly lead friends to find they are not alone though they can't physically see, their loved one now an angel above, never to leave.

Like the rhythm of the Pilates woodpecker my feet in harmony, the practice of patience as I seek my destiny. Eyes down viewing as far as my next step, only occasional glance up to what lies ahead. With the beat of time unfolding as it sees best, I am learning to let go and trust the rest.

Neither of us had patience as our strength, how often our mantra, "Not the destination," as a reminder to our restless souls trying to contain. So much to see, the urging to continually *do*, sitting still withheld from exploring not a favorite for you. My soul feeling the same, so many experiences it craves.

The closer to center, the more focus required to run an even gait; the closer to complete self-acceptance, the more excited to hurry the pace. Our roles reversed now, you are pulling back an imagined leash. "Slow down the urge to hurry, Mom," you whisper to me. "I am in the now of this run," the mantra repeats. A beginning, then more routine, with each step, increased steadiness, I breathe.

Your gentle reminder of what else you taught me, the moments of each day are extraordinary. In the anxiousness to achieve certain dreams, sometimes the quest watching for "bigger" happenings. You lead me back to us sitting in the yard, the sound of birds, the gentle breeze. You continue to flash moments when in harmony, when joy bursts forth feeling complete. Like a run when I whisper, "I need a sign," seconds later "gentleness" and "transformation" from the deer and butterfly. To some the moment simple, to my heart the significant event I seek. Affirmation you listen, you answer, with me always you will be.

My heart's restlessness slowing to match each step, no longer the urge to hurry to what lies ahead. Nature's "voice" I see and hear, trust and happiness replacing old habits of fear. Fallen from the tree outstretched in its orange and yellow array, its colors affirming "be joyful each day."

Gratitude, wholeness, excitement for what in due time could be. To confirm you know my heart, another messenger crossing paths with me. The blue heron steady in flight, methodical with each winged beat. Matching what now felt "peace and tranquility."

June 5, 2015

I strive to be a reflection of you, if I am someone else's mirror, your goodness is their view. You have led me to my own looking glass, to the shadows through time I had cast. When not yet brave enough, or not yet aware to see, in those times defense or judgment were protecting me.

Knowing an "old" habit is trying to awake, I search within for the culprit at play. You continue to bring Earth angels across my path to guide me, now that you know I am open to more discovery. Your nudge when one layer uncovered, then another, and a third layer as I stand at the mirror vulnerably bare. Shame has been an undergarment I wear.

You sent a silent messenger who could only speak with her eyes, slowly, quietly her nearing my side. Closer she walked, unafraid, a new friend in the make. She whispered, "Gentle compassion with others, with life, with yourself too. In addition, graceful determination I give to you." Her heart integrating with mine when our eyes locked for a few minutes' time. The deer unafraid, ever closer she drew; similar to Owl, an integration with my heart I knew.

As I let go of the self who feels shame, to accept that to

learn compassion, there first must be judgment and pain. And to judge another is the mirror of our own soul, in what we aren't yet ready to look into, our own self-loathe. As I recognize I still have more to unhide, slowly I find the bravery not to keep feelings locked inside. The image of the deer's eyes comes into my mind's sight, another message to heed, "When you begin to unconditionally love the all of you, to all others you will give unconditionally to."

So many gifts you've given for me to receive, my gratitude, dear Roo, most of all, you have given my heart to me. You entered my life when its beat was a faded sound. With your love, courage to let it open I found. You brought life to my soul's dying, you then died of this Earth that I would further live. My dear Roo, to the moon I love you, forever my special, special gift.

And, dear Roo, I no longer feel the gravity of death as I may have, thankful to you for showing me the promise that connection lasts. Death is rebirth, death can bring gifts, death is not good-bye; death holds purpose to make loss matter in life. As a friend courageously paid tribute to her husband now her angel above, witness to the beauty in her fragility and heartbreaking love. I know she is about to enter the darkest days of her life, and I know she will get through to the "other side." In the shakiest foundation she now knows, is her strength and a most certain hope.

June 13, 2015

Quietness used to be a safety net, a retreat inward before I could see, that the feeling of loneliness was because my heart not unleashed. The inner girl wish that others would invite, include, or seek her company was a blindness to the opposite action she was creating. I can still feel the blanket of quietness wrapping itself tighter around me, so certain again I would never speak. Through the motions of each day, the outer shell moved, but inside silence grew.

I ponder what it was like for you, the stillness you were feeling, too. As your momma was feeling more lost with time's forward moves, your heart also broken in two. You were missing your big brother Hansey after he said, "I have reached readiness to let go." The depth of your sorrow I didn't fully know. And yet, your unconditional love so strong, your rise above your pain, to be the steady certainty as I tried to find my way. You knew before me this darkness purposeful, that soon I would awake, your quietness a teacher I would later emulate.

Now I hush as you taught me to do, that I can hear more clearly what you want me to. My heart no longer tries to hide, listening differently. Before when silent among others, it was feeling unworthy. Now, it listens for others who struggle to believe. When someone says, "Your message was just what I needed" or "Perfect timing," my heart in gratitude you helped me hear another in need. I was given the gift of you to lead me to loving me; now I am trying my best to be your reflection for others on their journey.

When your little sis gives a hug, I know it is more than her expressing love. In those seconds she lingers wrapped in an embrace, I hear her soul softly whisper, "Hold me just a little longer before the rush of the day. I am enough, right? Sometimes I feel unsure. Your assurance helps ease my fear." I know Ginger has much to teach me, but I also know our paths have joined to help her healing.

I close my eyes and feel you curled up against my legs and reflect on just how much you are a source of my strength. Like the image of two sets of footprints, and sometimes just one, I anticipate similar you and me on our runs. You carried my weary heart when I feared or lacked faith, your unconditional love guiding and assuring each step I'd take. You now know I am ready to help others through, in that same quiet, steady way representing you.

A lightness to my heart, no longer the sorrow and grief, comfort that we are still together, even though you're not physically seen. And true to you affirming you have taught me how to listen and seek, another message you send shows that my heart you read. Past the window it flies, circles, and flies back by with, "Mom, hi. The peace and tranquility in your heartbeat, as Heron I am the reminder always with you I am and will be."

June 18, 2015

Do angels shadow a baby before they take their first breath?
Are angels whispering days or weeks prior, "Get ready for the
best"? Messages abounding through the steps I take, a birth
into new life I feel I am about to make. I can't see what the
future holds, but I continue to hear your whisper, "Trust,
listen, let go." You are whispering to your little sis as well, my
Roo; her trust and her guardianship growing too.

Like color as your little sis, instant my heart's warmth at
their similar-ness. The fawn out of hiding after a torrential
rain, its momma close behind ensuring it safe. Not only their
whispers of compassion and gentle grace, but motherhood
and birth in their presence today. Nine months and a day since
I touched the last beat of your heart, but instead of an ending,
it has led to a start.

Ginger, my protector if your daddy's not by our side, her
bark alerting that for me she would bite. I held safe with her
watchful eye, much strength hidden in her tiny size. My physical protection not her only watch, just like if staying up too
late, she nudges "stop." She, the keeper of my mind when it
needs to rejuvenate, and sometimes in the night I believe she

also keeps negative spirits at bay. Her powerful knowing my spirit is ready to hear, her head across my neck, in the dark she softly says, "I love you, ssshhh, you rest. I'm here."

The laughter that travels from somewhere deep every morning; our "time for breakfast then chase the bears away" routine. As alarm clock in her pounce, kiss, and song she sings; her influence of my childlike giggles of joy in each daily greet. I enjoyed mornings before the gift of your precious sis, but a whole new level found now—a pure bliss. I look for the moon each morning we step outside, the sky's comfort you are still nearby. But now I look, not only trusting you are right beside me, but trusting in signs of your enjoyment at your sis's glee.

She is capturing my left arm, Roo, or maybe she is repairing the right. I didn't think it possible to love so much another time. She so patiently, so gracefully, watches me; her eyes reflecting her heart's need. "I know you see me, Momma, I know you love me so. There is even more we could show each other, though. You can continue to teach me how Nature speaks, how my big sister and angels bring us answers we need. And I can continue to show you how to quietly be, through stillness greater your ability to see."

Serenaded this week by angels, filling me with your love; with each message deeper my affirmation of trust in all things, in self, in being "more than enough." A moment takes place and you are there in cheer. "Yes! Exactly! Trust what you hear." A widening of the heart, a taller stand, closer, closer still, I reach out my hand. The doorknob to a new path is within reach, the door about to swing, and I in awe of this feeling; right where I should be—no fear where you lead.

My love for Ginger, my love of this beautiful life, my newfound love in me. You danced around us. "Keep transforming. I am so proud of how you are both unfolding." Our hearts continuing to integrate, leaning on one another to teach. Again a reminder of motherhood and souls that bond, as the butterfly circles Ginger and me. A second time graced with the fawn and momma deer, this time so very near. Seventy-five feet or less from our home, "gentleness with your precious gift this baby" I have been entrusted to love.

The birds of red, of blue, of orange bellies and black wings too. Each a messenger of self-love, of faith in what is felt. Of beauty in loss the promise held. Another messenger you sent to me; the honor of writing for him a life story. Initially a stranger, quickly a newfound friend; a grateful reminder and graceful walk near his life end. When the words written gave my new friend peace, when I saw in his eyes that same look of soaking in life before his time to leave. Not sorrow that soon he would be an angel above, but an appreciation of all the extraordinary that life consists of. In your message, "Right where you are at, you are supposed to be," in my sight magically, yet surely, Hawk's visit to me.

Oneness with self, a trust in the relativity of time and space; trust the doors ahead will be reached, no longer an anxious race. Exhilarated by the unfolding, faith in the uncertainty, immense love for this preciousness walking with me. And then here you are, kisses on my forehead and Ginger's too, dancing with us. "Keep going, keep transforming. Mom, always beside you." The butterfly swooped and circled and gleefully bounced between. My amazing life, my Roo, Ginger, and me.

June 20, 2015

In that nothing coincidence way, always at the perfect time deliveries took place. As your health progressed in a direction we didn't want to face, as if on cue a package would arrive to brighten your daddy's day. The day the three of us whispered, "See you in new ways," another package outside the garage to await. Accessory or necessity, each ordered part, the things that would help the motor to start. Your daddy's lifeline to hope and faith, his dream coming together to counter his pain.

You had whispered, "Reread our talks during our last shared days. I will help you not feel overwhelming sorrow. It will be okay." Affirmation you would guide me through revisiting, past the window you sent blue heron messaging, "peace and tranquility." September fourth, September fifth, closer toward the twelfth I continued to read. My dear Roo, these priceless memories, how you taught me to listen, to watch, to just *be*. An appreciation of time without hurry.

The pages opening safety boxes of the heart—like watching the twitch of your nose smelling near and far. Your eyes reflecting all that you were drinking in, capturing your favorite sights before your next role would begin. Among the messages you wanted me to see, there on the pages the love from your daddy. His assurance we would be okay without you physically at our side, his promise of our future and the new experiences we would find.

There in written form what you have continued to remind me, your daddy and I loving a four-legged soul again, your expectation and my promise to keep. Working on the car not your daddy's interest nor priority, until your little sis joined our family. Your little sis has been your daddy's assistant at times as I know you see; she serves as his garage mascot, keeping him company. To make sure your daddy had fun with this, often when he's working, she would give him a kiss. Daddy's giggles not only communicating enjoyment, but also "Ginger, I love you," honoring your wish he open his heart to another, too. And your little sis standing with such pride, not fearful of the motor noise in its start for the first time.

Your daddy's eyes reflecting such happiness at what was about to take place, the realization of his goal six years in the make. From the garage to the driveway, then to the road, your daddy's first test-drive as your little sis and I watch him go. Then my turn for a ride—slowly we head up the drive. With the same laughter that erupts when your little sis wakes me, from a deeply joyous place I laugh from the passenger seat. The intensity of the glee twofold, and I am not sure which the greater of two. Seeing your daddy's exhilaration or feeling your love, my beautiful Roo.

We are where you and your daddy both said we would be; we are giving another love and we are experiencing new things. We have survived the time I wasn't sure I could. Confirmation of what you told me September fourth, fifth, that morning— that I would.

I think I will come to associate your daddy's old car as symbolic of light and hope, which is ironic considering its jet-black dark color, sleek and bold. As the human part of our souls work on healing the soreness of cracked-open hearts, the car is a symbol that it doesn't stay dark. You are the guardian who is still orchestrating dreams to come true, your love unending, our beautiful Roo.

June 21, 2015

You continue to lead me to circles of *then* through the lens of *now*. An awareness yet again I have found. You know how I believe; others enter our lives for a moment, a season, or for a lifetime, purpose in why we meet. The summer party, a gathering of friendships that space and time have interjected into since last seen; a reunion to affirm the "season" of my life's journey. The party held by those who will walk the duration of life with me; other friends there a shorter-term gift received.

On our daily run, you gently lead me through the layers as I ponder actions and reactions, healing and letting go. Carrying me, and grounding me, as I searched deeper to know. As you continue to teach me how to hear, more aware to insincerity; a smile not from the heart I "read" instantly. In walking away with a certain defense, a triggered anger in me, you nudged, "You know the anger is within, not against the greeting you received."

You brought to mind a shared memory, a time when I had given to the greeter my heart openly. Was it hurt that giving of myself so vulnerably was not viewed as a gift to the other to safely keep? Or was I mad at the self of me as I was then, the self who hadn't yet fallen in love with who she wanted to be? Did I wish this self had felt "more than enough" so she wouldn't have searched for others who could? Did I wish this self hadn't looked to those who never would?

Another mile marker, another layer reached, recognition of my gravitation to certain personalities. Certain life teachers had been sought who represented a familiarity, who reflected a comfort in childhood feelings. As I unconsciously moved, searching for the center of me, traits like my father's I would seek. A little girl longing to hear, "I am proud of you exactly as you are", searching for others to play that part.

The only one who could give me those words was standing beside me, the one in the mirror a reflection back

Me.

You whisper, "Complete the forgiveness that you didn't know then what you have come to know, I bring you these circles so that you can further let go. The more that you release the 'old self' attachments to what was, the more grounded you will be in 'enough.' The less that you think of external reaction to who you are showing you want to be, the more you will hear others who need your help to believe. Mom, as you reread what your heart did not forget in our promise made, together our communication to others, 'trust, don't be afraid.'"

Nearing the end of the run, you call to me, "Always with you, your guardian, together we are a team. Keep listening as you are, and trust where the path will lead. Mom, I am proud of you. To the moon, always, you and me." Two Hawks poised in the tree, representative of you, dear Roo, always with me.

June 26, 2015

I felt you with me standing in our place, where we had stood
that morning of our last Earth together day. Rose petals in my
hand to toss into the breeze, the feeling of you right next to me.
Gratitude for the sensation, tears of love, and then a moment,
or more, wishing for more than you above. Maybe because the
path now cleared to further see, or maybe you like the fun of
affirming for me. Later on, a walk with your little sis, my familiar call, "I need a sign." Minutes later, at my step, an angel's
feather I find.

You have led me to certain memories, as a little girl with
a chocolate dessert I am about to eat. I am back in time with
grandparents, their love of me, and then I am with Great
Grandma as she places in my hand a slice of ice cream. Her
eyes shine "you are special," and in her view I am enough;
another showering me with love. In youth, as adult, more
unconditionally I receive, a mother's abundant giving of her
heart, and of home-cooked food, to me. Food as a comfort one
puzzle piece; as the memories replay you whisper, "Hidden"
and "Speak."

Buttons pushed in my mind, fast-forward, pause, rewind.

Like a staircase winding down, closer to the last door, you are gently guiding me toward my core. I am that little girl—I am safe, I am quiet, striving not to be seen. Feeling "less than," scared, unworthy, my secret I keep. I am in the comfort of my grandparents' home, able to keep my thoughts and my voice locked deep, accepting food as their expression of love, food filling the hunger to speak.

I am an adult, I am safe, I am finding the courage to be seen. Feeling "more than enough" much more frequently, no longer afraid to share what I believe. Accepting some will not share my same views, recognizing I fulfill purpose if I let people choose. If I am trying to honor everyone else, I short-change the trueness you have taught me; I am actually disloyal to everyone if not fully seen. Our reason for interacting only partially realized, the lesson plan incomplete if I hide.

Additional steps taken in showing what I believe, letting go of old habits and old feelings. No longer that girl who strived to be like others instead of my own authenticity, now my voice showing up written or verbally. Your encouragement, your pride: "Mom, don't keep you inside." After practicing an unveiling of more for others to see, you land inches from the next step of my feet. Dragonfly as spirit from above, my dear Roo, encouraging me "do more of this" with your love.

June 29, 2015

Outstretched wings soar into view, your message of love, our dear Roo. Twice you were there with a message, "I love you, family. Watching over you, I will always be." Keeper of my heart and what it needs, appearing as affirmation, acceptance of my soul's peace.

We had lounged lazily as the day began, relishing a day not fully planned. Our drive relaxing, my heart celebrating another layer released. Feeling content, proud of another step forward, a little more unveiling "this is me." Your first visit in circle as you begin to slow, a glide over the roof you know as home. "It's okay to feel so complete," as the sun glistens against your beautiful white wings. My heart in extra skip, your happiness at my pure bliss.

The second visit a day later, Ginger, your daddy, and me, on the way to the trail for an evening walk: our family. The turkey the first catch of the eye, his reflection of my gratitude for my amazing life. As I wrapped in the message of "blessings," there from the right another message in Hawk's beating wings. "Keep going forward. Listen to the whisper that guides what you hear. With each subtle shift, a significant purging of fear."

It was a gentle push to try something new, when shedding the comfort of "old" what the soul desires to do. A new section of trail not before visited with Ginger at my side—the last time for me during a race to the finish line. Nor does the trail section contain a memory with you; the last time right here was solo as I ran through. My only flashback in time, celebration when I saw mile marker nine. It was my first ultra, thirty-three-and-one-half miles to achieve. I shouldn't say you were not there, my dear running mate; for beside me you are with every step I take. New exploration with your little sis, finding a parallel to life in this.

Ready to embrace the new, being open to what is not yet in view. The mile markers not easily seen, nor memorized to know distance before the next one reached. Ginger and I embracing the *now*, trusting our stepping, knowing *when* no longer our need. If the mile marker doesn't appear earlier than we might have planned, our sign that flexibility and determination go hand-in-hand. Not focused on the comfort of the markers we usually see, hearing and seeing—really looking—at our surroundings. The woods, the trees, the sun peeking through the green leaves; do I notice on the "old" trail with the same intensity? Or am I finally listening: "go explore new things"?

Your little sis so quickly taking a leap of faith, her history unknown but her heart's protection could have kept her at bay. New trails, visiting somewhere not familiar, adventure with your daddy and I; Ginger doesn't care as long as one or both of us in her sight. Your daddy and I blessed her heart quickly given to us, near immediacy we received her faith and trust. I had thought Ginger the student of how to trust and let go, I as her teacher to help her soul grow. But perhaps reversed who is the guide and who is continuing her affirming; Ginger enforcing unconditional trusting.

You had led me to the edge, and the free fall began, your sureness on my feet I would land. I am confident you whispered in Ginger's ear, "Soon, you will unite with who you have been searching to find. Momma and Daddy will take great care of you. You will be all right." Or maybe you also told her, "Okay, now you take it from here. Momma has opened wide her heart, her eyes, her ears. Keep her listening, keep her seeing, keep her in faith in what she can't see. And while I watch from above, you my Earth partner, keep her protected for me."

July 1, 2015

She sleeps, ever so softly an occasional snore from somewhere deep. Ever my protector, lying beside me, her ear alert, her heart listening. A blend of all three like soul, body, and mind; one cannot feel without hearing—one cannot hear without sight. Each gets attention to strengthen the other two, your predominance awaking me to *see*, my beautiful Roo. With the turns and angles of her ears, precious Ginger teaching me further how to hear. With my heart growing in bravery to open wide, together both of you guiding me to shine.

Like a race that takes me to that spent place, shortened sleep quieting my busy mind over the past days. It is a periodic routine creating this tired state, for my mind to slow and my soul to come awake. A runner will talk of that many mile "high," the same feeling in that most depleted state the most felt alive. When I help my mind quiet, my heart hears more clear, in tune to another who may need help with their fears.

You may whisper a name or send a messenger to me; awe and affirmation in the response received. A moth to whisper, "Tell Mom again, always by her side." His mom's response, "I, too, had a moth visit me. I wondered if he was saying, 'Hi.'"

An awe that you utilize me to help give another hope; that together we can message after physical death doesn't mean the one left on Earth is now on their own. And gratitude for the affirmation I am hearing accurately, what to say to who may have a heart in need.

In that felt moment, I hear you call, "I love you, Mom. So very proud that you kept your heart, ears, and eyes open to notice and receive. You are carrying forward what we learned together. You are making it matter that in the middle of our shared life, cancer decided to intervene. We talked of the purpose, we talked of how I would help you, we talked of together being messenger for others to *see* too. Hope and faith that it is never good-bye. A physical death doesn't remove someone from our side." Your screech as you fly over me, beautiful Hawk soaring as my forever guardian—the safe keeper of my heart. Always together, our hearts never to part.

July 4, 2015

I ponder how far in advance your soul knew that your time on Earth would end soon. Though time is limitless and "soon" could be further away, did you know somewhere deep that you were nearer a last day? Were you hearing the whisper "maximize time"? Or perhaps you weren't yet awake to the signs.

I looked up the exact time your messenger flew past my view, in humble awe seeing the brown and whites of its wings and tail as it flew. Grateful for your visit, in awe that I heard you softly whisper, "Hi," at the exact flash of seconds you passed by. Vivid and so close in reach. Because you taught me heightened sight and sound, with open arms Hawk's message my receipt.

I walk back through time before sickness, seizures, and a sometimes slower pace, when I sensed coming our way would be a life change. I didn't necessarily think it would be with you, or was it protection before I was ready to hear exactly what the soul knew? As I stay more aware to hear your little sis, that I would have been in tune to your health sooner my wish. Just when I long to have heard your message before this, you gently remind me I did. "Mom, remember you dreamed me before we met, before I entered this life; even then our souls connected awaiting the right time."

It is the seven-year anniversary when your grandpa left Earth too; thinking of what his soul whispered before his heart the avenue. Your catalyst cancer, his a heart in two, both willing to give such love in what you each decided to do. Sometimes we do not begin to fully know the gifts we receive until we are tested to let go. Through your grandpa's passing I found love, through your letting go a deeper part of my soul.

"To the moon and back, Momma, and more than just me. You know many are with you so lovingly." As your little sis and I greet the morning, I hear your messenger speak, its owl hoot calling, "With you I am. Continue to trust what you hear and see."

I am not sure how much your grandpa was aware what his last day would be, before his heart arrested its remaining beats. But I do know his soul said, "Not yet, a few more hours before purpose complete. Wake up long enough to see each of your girls, then you will come above in peace." What your grandpa thought before not important; what matters the gifts he gave me. Seven years ago he left me with certainty; "not enough" as his daughter was my belief. Through you as my guide, dear Roo, I came to see, your grandpa and I shared a commonality. Your grandpa didn't believe he was "enough" at the core of his heart; we were in sync, not far apart. And at the deepest of his soul he was giving what I had always hoped to receive, unconditional love for me. Now, I can fully see: I actually was always "enough" in your grandpa's view of me; yet his refrain from telling me and my own believing reflected our own insecurities.

A kiss blown to you as you shine the moon at me, gratitude you will never leave. Additional gratitude that you led me to this abundant sense of peace and harmony. I am still in awe, dear Roo, of your ability to find me in the darkness, though I know that's your specialty. Just like the moon that brightly shines, you knew there was light you could help me find. For a moment I wish I could physically touch you as I reach for your little sis; the feel of you I sure do miss. But then you softly whisper, "Mom, how blessed you truly are, surrounded by much love on Earth and above, always our joined hearts."

July 5, 2015

Every so often she turns to me, her smile as her eyes look to see. Sometimes I feel like I've been caught, somewhere else lost in thoughts. Each glance brings me back to current steps, ensuring I am not focused too far ahead. You have told me more than once your little sis is my grounding, she a foundation to keep me patient for the future unfolding. Each time she looks to ensure I agree with where she leads, strength and harmony for my footing achieved.

Your daddy noticed too, how the four of them lingered in our view. Four crows to communicate "keep seeing the magic of each day," yet there seemed to be more you were guiding them to say. There in the morning, midday, and at night; again the next day for our sight.

Like a code deciphering, you continued to give more clues, "longevity" and "grounding" the consistent words from you. The sandhill cranes singing next to me, "abundant time" as they kept me company. Pedaling miles as part of training; thirteen weeks to our big run and counting. Then your urging Ginger and I drive back down the road, a double check was it a bird that had not flown? With a second look, the opportunity to carry a turtle from harm's way; again the message "grounded in place."

Knowing an anxiousness to get "there" my tendency, pondering on where I am overly rushing. The upcoming race in a week, building an excitement for our September feat. Events on the calendar I'm looking forward to; perhaps in the eagerness for those, too much a forward view. You take my thoughts to a conversation recently, a way I was able to assist through sharing what I believe. Pain no longer hindering the ability to vulnerably be, now "on the other side" as an inspiration to another in need. And then the awareness washes over me; I was able to help another's uneven balance because of my grounding.

The messages you've sent haven't been as much about "keep working on your foundation for you aren't there yet." They have been about this more: "keep going, you are starting to live what you had been striving to get." My old habits would look at what I am not yet doing perfectly; your reminders celebrating are also key. A shift in my running, feeling the focus on the end point falling away; embracing the *now* of each step I take. The momentary fears of "can I?" "will I?" "what if?" now replaced with "I will, my way okay, I can do this."

Not yet seeing, but hearing through the trees, at the start of my longer run, your call to me. At the same place you perched a couple of weeks ago, both of you awaiting my approach. On the limbs your guardianship unwavering. "You are hearing correctly, have a good run, always with you watching. Have fun." A few miles later, my return; in the same tree your Hawk love assured.

July 10, 2015

The where's not what matters, she is along for the ride. Her focus that she is by our side. Another family adventure she gets to partake, sights and sounds she will encounter in new ways. In the sand her wonderment and her leaps of joy and childlike surprise; her never-before experience tears to my eyes. Not knowing for certain but my heart whispers, "The same thing." This is the happiness a parent feels giving their child wings.

Your daddy and I are not new to the upper north views, but we never experienced them with you. Home, your sanctuary, your comfort zone, where you kept watch over until our return home.

I am immersed in our time as family. I am eager for the reason that prompted our traveling. A trail race awaits, sixteen miles among the trees; and I know each step, you will be with me. Closer to your little sis, she continues to draw me to the new. I am learning to replace my irregular heartbeat with peace each time I think of you.

I know you are so happy for your daddy, little sis, and me; that what we are sharing is exactly your plan, where you continue to lead. In your whispers of trust as you led me to our edge, you had assured me all would be well in what lies ahead. True to life in the opposites that balance when they meet, faith through the biggest void,

I now feel complete.

July 12, 2015

The crowd cleared to the left and to the right; there you stood in full sight. You ran over a hill—for a moment you weren't seen. Then back with your familiar "ready to go" energy. You carried back a collection of something, what exactly not clear. But I remember the feeling of your protection from strangers not to come near. I called your name, you responded with my matching joy and pride; then both of us to a door, entering inside.

Moments later, I awoke from the dream, grateful for our shared time and your message for me. The trail race I'd be starting a few more hours away; it would be a success, you with every step I take.

Your little sis is smaller, a puppy's nose trying to decipher the scented leaves. She and I curled up in the sun's warmth yet we were also in the shade of trees. We fell asleep embraced in peace, your little sis quieting the restlessness in me. She my second visitor in a dream, in the time between your visit and three minutes before the alarm was due to ring.

A third messenger you sent to greet, gray Fox to our left as your daddy and Ginger walked to the packet pickup with me.

"You will do well. Luck is beside you today." Excitement and trust in each step to the starting line I take.

The water belt not destined to make the finish with me, in the first mile contemplating where it I could leave. In that moment, her sweet whine, "I love you, stay safe, I will miss you until you cross the finish line." Your little sis and Daddy across the street; perfect timing to take the belt from me.

One small pocket already carrying what I might need, not much room remaining for anything else to bring. The locket in my hand, the locket in honor of you, carried last year after you became an angel above and carried in Greece too. The fear of losing it strong, trust you are with me even stronger than an object that isn't you. And, strongest the sound, "Honor Ginger," encouragement from you, dear Roo. "Mom, she loves you, she is your purpose to lead you forward as we both know. I will run beside you soul to soul. Your Ginger, your 'precious' is now your Earth gift; let her be beside every step of this."

Switching back and forth, up and still up more. Mile after mile my spirit soars. My eyesight starting to align with the tops of trees, not so long ago running like this not reality. The sweetness that an up usually has a down that awaits, the running comrades, "you got this," while we all persevere through the race.

Partway through your daddy and Ginger there with "Good job" and hugs for me. My cheerleaders, my supporters unconditionally. Your daddy hasn't changed as I know you see; still his happiness when he feels he has helped give all of my dreams to me. Even if trail running's not his passion like your momma's is, he is glad to support adventurers like this.

Across the finish injury free, blessed beyond measure for health and family, and the people that in every experience we are given the chance to meet. Kept safely from injury, kept in the *now* of the run, more people met, more puzzle pieces to fit into the picture called my life. Ginger's hug, your daddy's love-filled eyes, and in my heart to the moon and back where you reside.

July 13, 2015

For you, sharing toast with Daddy, squirrels, and definitely our running too. Anything to do with the word "go," my beautiful Roo. And scouting for critters or treats each morning your insistent routine. And dirt roads so you could scout while in the Jeep's front seat.

For your Hansey, it was tennis balls. For your little sis, I haven't yet identified what grabs hold of her most of all. All things loved to do, none of them harmful to your big brother or you. But oh, a sweet addiction in each your relentless pursuits; some of your daddy's and my favorite memories shared as they pour through. Tennis balls, balls dropped in water so as not to swim away when the water drank, sticks, an occasional turtle somersaulted until it could begin the laborious walk to the lake's bank.

I, too, an addict, I have come to recognize, a sweet pursuit of this found feeling inside. I have thought my quest toward the center of me symbolic like that set of spiral stairs walked downward to somewhere deep. As I proclaim to the one in the mirror what I now crave, I reflect on what it has replaced. Now, the symbolism of a stairway being built upward, sturdier as its height grows, each step reflecting a habit being let go.

At the most exhausted state, in mind, body, or soul, it is then I am most alive, where felt the most hope. My spirit traveled through its darkest state. Walking without feeling the steps made. Depression's fog covering all but the fragment of the soul that knew; amazing things await the other side of this tiredness if I keep pushing through. So many gifts would not have been found if not for that time; gratitude for every painful moment that has given such goodness to my life.

Like my soul able to walk with grace through our last Earth days. If not for the time prior, far more struggles in my ability to honor you, dear Roo. These last months would have been harder to carry forward the trust you have led me to.

Periodically I quiet the mind with a shortage of sleep; in that opposite way of learning, often in tiredness the most clarity to *see*. And the races an exhilarating tiredness that brings such harmony. My body a blend of stillness with the urge to continue, my soul filled with immense belief. No room for "cannot" once again proven when completing the race; hope, can, and will at the start carried to the finish line step I make.

I had been addicted to the comfort of feeling "not enough." Though I longed for more, it was much easier for my mind to repeat, "unworthy of love." As I am finding self-acceptance, the fed habits are losing hold, no longer a euphoria felt to self-loathe. Now instead of the cycle that perpetuates "it must be true, not enough, see self, I told you," the cycle is gaining momentum: "Try, you can, believe; self, even if you stumble you are still more than enough to me."

Just as an addiction never leaves, I know this will be a lifelong evolution for me. Self-acceptance will be a habit I strive to strengthen, but now I have something special not had before.

sibility, and I know much more. Your gift of trust, the beauty found from pain, purpose in all things to gain. Even if now an angel above, never are those we love far away. And beside us on Earth are additional angels to guide our way.

July 19, 2015

In my hand the keeper of them all—the tubed ones with squeakers, the gray donkey, the lavender-and-yellow monkey—the memories recalled. They have held a place for ten months and a little bit more; I couldn't bear letting them go before. Now as I hold the box of your toys that you once tossed in the air, squeaked in excitement before a run, or briefly chewed; my heart at peace that if I let go of these, you I won't lose.

Purging and reorganizing throughout home not new, often you would watch as I created piles room by room. Tossing out, donating, and letting go, waves of openness felt in my soul. More gets purged, parallel to the deeper I walk to the center of me; no longer fearful I am losing love if I don't hold on to things.

A memory not recalled until this time's purging, the youth of school once pushed from memory. Craving to feel "enough," avoiding friendship and forgiveness with the self who hadn't known how, letting go of association with letters and pictures I found. Not then able to accept life is about the experience of learning, not yet taught by you. Still averse to running, still hiding from view. Then it was a run from, far away from the mirror reflection, from the pain; not yet discovering the thirst to run to, open arms to embrace. One card didn't make the toss back then, a gift awaiting me now from a no-longer-in-touch friend. The pieces of self I now value in knowing I am for the world around me, even then—yes, even then per the card—they were a part of who I was trying to be.

Now I wonder what the words were that were ripped from their pages years ago. Nothing is coincidence, choice not to regret what was let go. Instead my heart sends a wave of love to the girl that was me. "I am sorry for the pain so strong certain things you couldn't keep. But oh, my dear Chris, how far we have come in our life journey. Each step taken to make us who we want to be. What great things await us in living that we can't yet fully see."

Gratitude now the guiding force in every room; peace and eagerness also behind what I choose. No longer governed by pain, no longer raw and afraid to face. Grateful for the abundance I have, and have had, thankful for each and every life lesson plan. No strong memory of making this cup; apparently it held trinkets of Dad's, a binding of far-apart love.

There is always more than what we think we see, and often we are the same though we think we are feeling differently. Multiple years when we couldn't communicate; the letter that sealed silence's fate. A mug that rested on his dresser tied to one end of a string; memories locked into a cedar chest across the divide my link. Hearts are bound through time and space, even when communication is absent and divided, unable to find a common place. For a brief moment, a readiness to let the mug go in the purging of what I no longer need. But then like the tiny stuffed dog that holds the corner of a drawer, this mug was meant to stay with me. This mug is only an object, but wrapped around it are imprints of hands—part of some-one who I can now see, as best he could from his own "not enough," he loved me.

Dear Roo, just as I make your desire matter going forward, that I live as you taught me. I know that I am to do the same, the purpose of his teachings. He lived a full life not fully coming to know, he didn't feel "more than" in every portion of his soul. His hope that I would break that cycle and pay forward that others might also believe, as each of us are—we are worthy. Through your gift of teaching me to hear now another whisper soft but clear. This time not just you, but someone else near. "Kit, words are hard for me to voice aloud. So many times I wanted to; please know I am so proud of you."

This round of purging and letting go complete, I am filled with peace. My guardian beside me; you above. I am surrounded by immense abundance, I am

Enough.

July 24, 2015

Her hug speaks volumes of immense love and of vulnerability. "I adore you, I get afraid, I vow to keep watch, please never let go of me." In her linger my heart listens closely; does she need a hug of equal adoration or to be comforting? Sometimes with eyes closed I have to remember she has four feet, the hug feeling childlike in its embracing. You led me to a widening heart, to opened expression of what is felt from places deep. Of your little sis you must be so proud, her purpose to continue expansion within me.

Certain I would feel what others have said in their grieving, never again to love as strong, no possibility. Moment by moment you lengthen the heart string that ties me tightly to you, encouragement to not weave you into all that Ginger and I do.

"She matters," you whisper as I reach. "This should be about Ginger only

for the Christmas tree." Hansey had his own ornament, his name to display, and one for you, a different style and shape. Recently both seen again in the purging, reorganizing, balancing weekend feat; one for Ginger a definite need. What to make, paint, create? Decisions, fun decisions with a special date. A birthday celebration with a niece to fuel her artistic soul, perusing options for the projects that grab the most hold. In my hand the ornament, then second thoughts fill me; the nudge stronger, louder. "Pick the paw ornament—this one the need. Not the owl ornament, nor the word plaque 'believe.'" Letting go. Letting in. Letting the heart lead.

The paws pink, the first days your sis was home my memories; now well-worn, dirt-smudged, traceable imprints across floors she leaves. Pastel colors speaking, "pureness," speaking "healed," speaking "unconditional acceptance and love." Without words, but the clear message "you are enough."

Each of us as artists for the day, in silence a similar theme at play. No longer seeing my niece as a younger version of someone else I know, no longer afraid of what it would mean of you to release my hold. If I had let go, you wouldn't be as near; if I let go, the younger version of me would have gotten too close, I used to fear. You as perfection teaching how to become the best of me; this younger self-reflection flawed, "less than," unworthy. Every one of the moments you and I shared purposeful and mostly pain free; this person in pain much of her life, this person as me.

I had the realization before that I was seeing my niece through the eyes of who I had been and didn't like. That had opened the door to let in healing's light. Final closure often takes place when new memories are made, when time spent with another for a moment or a day. Who didn't know she once held the shadow reflection I found the courage to face. No longer seeing her as a mirror of who I used to be, no longer projecting my childhood feelings for her to receive.

You, a reflection of my soul, my guardian leading me

bravely to the mirror. Gently you taught me to begin to love who appeared. Step by step acceptance, gratitude, and release, the younger self no longer pushed away from her role in helping make me, me. I let go to love her unconditionally. And side-by-side without a word yet so much being spoken as we explored our artistry, my heart grateful and bursting in love to have such a special and beautiful niece.

Like you, Ginger will help me far greater than what I can teach in turn; but as I embrace making myself matter, I can be teacher to help your little sis learn. Letting the heart take my hand, guide my feet; trusting, giving permission to honor the inner voice that says, "This is right for me." Easier to tell others that when you honor yourself everyone else gains, for the very best of you can then be given away. Harder to release what has haunted each step I did not dare take; others will think selfish if my needs and dreams a priority made. With your gift of sight, Ginger's gift to *hear* and together your gifts to feel and know, I am bravely paying heed to your message "Continue to practice how to fully show." "We know your heart," you guide the messengers to remind me; "Not selfish but with loving intent you strive to be. Keep being you, 'enough' you are. Let the world see."

July 29, 2015

It has been some time since I looked into this set of trees, remembrance of, and hope for a glimpse I'll see. The owl you and I talked with, later you sent to me; forever imprinted in my heart those powerful meetings.

It is a training day adding miles to these legs, the "big" race eight weeks away. Nearing the end goal, seven miles more to go, your messengers affirming the feelings coursing through my soul. Feeling content, feeling excited, feeling grateful too; turkeys across my path whispering, "Blessings to you."

Relishing that spent feeling starting to take hold, knowing *can* and *will* in the remaining two miles to go. My silent partner, my guardian, vigilant watch over me; there as reminder always at my side, your majestic poise in that tree. Your strength my steadiness, confirmation that this race is meant to be; through Hawk your message, "Mom, near the finish you are, keep listening, continue to *see*. Mom, keep trusting."

The shadow of the moon catching more of my eye, more frequent wake-ups in the night. Nearer to that 4:00 a.m. window my heart is stirring me awake. You are communicating, "Stand quietly, step softly, trust each step you feel urged to take. You can't see ahead but only your dreams; you are being led to where you want and need to be. Shhh. Still that restlessness, the impatience, replay where I affirmed the power of believe, all the ways things have fallen into place perfectly."

You became my angel above as the leaves began their transformation, when it was their time to also depart, to make room for new growth, extended branches, a firmer foundation—in the near future spring's new start. Leaves are gently dancing and dropping through the sky, clusters dotting paths I travel by. Many speak in disbelief that summer is racing past, unsettled in time, moving incredibly fast. I am in awe that we are nearing September twelfth again, that one year—soon—it has been. Like the season of fall, my soul has been allowing the bareness to unfold. Am I knocking on spring's door now, readying for the new to take hold?

Change is in the air, and I am no longer afraid. A greater trust of what lies ahead, of what life may ask me to face. Will moments of uncertainty still pause my breath? I hope so, for it is only then that I grow through that out-of-comfort stretch. We made a plan, your knowledge of our purpose greater than what I could then see. I've done my best to honor what you desired to teach. You whispered, "Trust, I will hold your hand, even when I you can't physically see." To the moon and back, my dear Roo, among why I love you—how much you have loved me.

You taught me how to love unconditionally; you led me to the start of a circle to complete. I knew love for others, but it was given away with a price; walls of defense or searching for voids to be filled, the wrong "receivers" I would find. Nature the lifeline, messengers communicating "we hear you, we love you, you are worthy." With each step to self-accepting along with you they would lead. Now with a view from "enough" hearing differently: compassion for others' perspectives, no longer internalizing their words as "unworthy." Shifting yet further to hear messengers in new ways, words I might be able to speak to inspire others with faith.

I am nearing the start and finish where the ends meet; soon I will step away from this circle to a new opening. Where it leads I do not know, "soon" the when undefined; only an inner whisper from you saying, "All as it should be, all in due time." You and I made a pact to give ourselves a year; now, you are signaling that time is drawing near. And I can feel you lengthening the string that binds us, that I might expand, explore, and experience new things. You knew I could, and now you continue to lead; together we are moving toward the finish that every part of me will always believe.

I used to fear before a race, anxious with each training run before the day. Now I am practicing with an eager certainty. I can and will, my heart beats. With my guardian angel above, my Earth angel also my lead, and with someone else very special—

Me.

August 2, 2015

She holds me close, a blend of assurance I will not leave and as my guardian held in her safety. A bold bravery around others, a quiet soul when her family not near; her loyalty to her greatest loves far stronger than her self-fears. She the teeter to balance the tottering me, the moments when courage more comfortable behind the scenes. A readiness to no longer crawl unnoticed under the TV, yet speaking without apology still part of my learning. Bolder on my own in what I think; hesitant with others—old habits run deep. Your little sis teaching me strength to voice out loud. To help your little sis know she is loved even when by herself my vow. Our oppositeness will help us each grow through the steps we take, Ginger and I each other's brave.

Forty days remain, three hundred and twenty-five days have rushed by; at least more often than not time has seemed to fly. I trusted your assurance I would be okay, that you would still be with me though you couldn't physically stay. As you were guiding me to befriend trust I didn't then know how deep; that trust has many layers if we are willing to see. You guided me to a ledge, you whispered, "Follow me. Mom, just wait, the best will come to be."

I pause for a moment during another day of our training, to my right, high among the open sky, outstretched and soaring wings. Not as Hawk, but your symbolic messaging, "Keep looking from a broader perspective, keep stretching to see, gracefully, with ease, patience, peace." Another prayer to you, "Closer that I can capture your flight in a picture's view." Not nearer, you decide, but now there are two. Standing grounded in place, letting impatience subside, trust that toward me your messenger will glide. From the left, a third with those beautiful wings, your message, "Faith you will be given what you want and need. Be open to the variation—along with patience is flexibility."

Images of others you bring to mind, showing me the ways I trust others part of my life. Certainly your daddy, from the moment voiced, "I will," then "I do," not knowing then love has such incredible depth, learned through experience, as I learned with you. And of course Ginger, family, friends, and with coworkers and cotrustees—yes, perhaps trust not a shortage in what I hand others to receive. You keep whispering that someone else is waiting, that it is time to share and make a priority. "Mom, trust your own heart as much as you trust me." And a final remnant to let go and heal; in the mirror I declare, "You are not selfish in what you feel."

You gently remind me of the times I give but don't necessarily know through feedback the impact of this. You whisper, "Mom, you don't always hear, or you aren't always there to see, but you *know* it made a difference because you believe. You trust that you were hearing through angels what another wanted you to say or do. It is time to apply that same trust through the all of you. I'll continue to help the affirmation, but

Mom, meet me halfway. In yourself, continue to build your faith." The pace steadier, the mind's urge to pause less disappearing. I see your eyes sparkle in joy: "You are surrendering."

August 6, 2015

Certain you are catching each kiss blown to you, lately under the morning moon our rendezvous. To its radiance and back, my love, dear Roo.

The opportunity is not lost on me, the depth of meaning around its timing. Another part of the world a gift to see, this time Australia I will get to greet. Leaving on the day we near the end of one of our two goals and the day you became angel when I'll start for home. You and I will have completed for a second time the race that imprinted my vow to take a stand for me. We will have completed all but the last two pages of our shared story.

Experiencing the new during the one-year anniversary, when you and I had shared the most amazing end of your time on Earth before your time to leave. I will be starting for home three hundred and sixty-five days after our home broke in three. The day I arrive home three hearts reunited, three hearts as one family complete. It will be two weeks until your birthday and thirteen days until our race; when together we will complete what will be part of our last page.

You sent a messenger in the form of a friend, her words

resonating with me. "I want to get up every day doing what makes my heart sing." Her angst that when she felt most joy and value in what she achieved was not always found in her work setting. Still separated, she felt, work from her life; her heart searching for "more" to find.

I pause, I reflect, I am starting to see, just like your messengers of flight soaring above me. Higher they rise each time they come into view, a message affirming what you want me to continue. My heart has found a song that doesn't grow quiet now in fear, starting to recognize it has a purpose for others to hear. Melding into one, no longer separating; outside of and at work the same lyrics I am starting to sing, "This is me."

That familiar feeling is moving nearer toward me; that soon I will be letting go as you whisper, "It is time to leave." I know you will always be by my side, our hearts linked forever through space and time. You have opened my heart to trust what it hears and sees; you have ensured many angels are surrounding me. As we near one year, as we are nearer our "big race," you are whispering, "I have helped you put a foundation in place. Mom, it is time you live what I have helped you come to know. Now it is about practicing—you might stumble sure, but keep listening to your soul. Like your runs now, Mom, such surrendering; you are trusting each step you take. In yourself you believe."

Along the last mile of tonight's training, a team of your angels awaits me. "You are loved, so very loved. We wrap you in peace." Mourning doves as beacons on the power line next to me, your messengers mirroring my heart's harmony. Dear Roo, I am moving in the right direction, aren't I? I feel like I am stepping ever closer to that door—it's time.

There is a handle to reach, not a ledge and a required leap. I am excited running to it like a child who can't wait, not willing time to slow, no longer a breaking heart clinging to faith. The same familiar feeling to trust what I can't see, that on the "other side" will be incredible things. This time, dear Roo, I feel like I will step through the doorway and gently reach behind. Gracefully, gratefully, so very gratefully I will softly close the door on those chapters of my life. A deep breath as the sunshine kisses my cheeks. Here I am life. This is

Me.

"Exactly Mom, exactly! I am so proud of you. With you always. To and back the moon."

August 14, 2015

I am not sure how the scratch like the Z of Zorro took place, if a thorned weed or your little sis's nail when being carried away. Not a major scrimmage, not even a fight at all; your mom interjecting to avoid a brawl. Polite the request to keep the other four-legged tiny tot at bay; raised in demand the voice when onward it came.

Putting self between this stranger in its fur coat and your little sis. Focusing to avoid either "child" getting bit. When near the heels of your little sis my view narrowing significantly, my only thought to ensure Ginger's safety. The other no longer near, until it found a second wind, eager to be friend or boss to your little sis. Scooped into my arms so as not to take a chance; carrying your little sis to quietness without a second glance.

The depth of my love, a mother's deep; I would lay down my life if the need. My heart felt that strongly for you; for your little sis—caught off guard that I have the same view. The encounter not that dangerous that lives were on the line, but reflection in the intensity felt inside. When I would say, "Cut off my right arm," that "someday" you would have to leave, you intertwined through the all of me. I always felt I would die for you if I had to step in front of harm's way. I anticipate parents of human babes feel the same. And that I feel the same powerful love for your little sis I didn't think a possibility; my heart in gratitude your encouragement that I kept that heart opening. Near a year later, I can still hear you tell me as we sat outside those last days, "It will be hard for you and Daddy but you have too much to not give it away. Mom, another will need what I have had: a good home and so much love. Your heart will hurt but honor me by sharing with another who needs to know they are enough."

Laying down one's life for another in many forms it can take; physically but also in unconditionally giving ways. You gave your life that I would come to know, a deeper ability to trust even when I can't see ahead life's road. We lay down a life for another when we allow vulnerability, to fully show who we are even if another might not like what they see. And we lay down a life when we let go of our own need, when we whisper, "It is okay, go in peace."

And into the sky above you went my dear Roo, to always guide me back and to the moon.

The path is being adorned with more as the steps I take; one, two, three, and the fourth this makes. You are whispering, "I will always be by your side but there are more than just me. Mom, so many want to help guide and lead. You are surrounded by angels who are eager to aid you in whatever you need. Think of them like your additional puzzle pieces to help complete. Just as you feel every person across your path is a piece that completes the picture of you, the angels I rally are also part of your portrait too. 'A team to get things done, and you can make your personal team as big as you choose'— what you tell others often, this very wise truth. So Mom, that 'ready' we talked about is more than just having a little sis; it is opening, allowing, 'letting in' so that you don't miss. More interlocking pieces are awaiting your gentle reach, your open arms to connect each."

The border not complete until my last breath, but anchors have been set. Corner posts that hold the foundation of me in place, that have—or continue to—aid in what is taking shape. Beautiful colors, perhaps a tattered edge; smoothness over time, awaiting links with the rest. You as a corner—actually, you may be nearer a centerpiece—and beside you another piece I need. Fanning out from each of you the picture yet to see, but with certainty because of both of you the picture incredibly, unconditionally, beautifully amazing.

More and more I see, all who you have surrounding me. Each in their own way whispering, "You are not alone, we walk with you."

Oh, so very right you were, my beautiful
so beautiful Roo.

That if I trusted, if I bravely let go, even more amazing the view of life I would come to know.

In the tree, a pillar, affirmation as guardian you will never leave; "Hello, Hawk, I will continue on life's run honoring your gift to see. And, thank you for always standing watch over me. When you majestically soar and glide, I will draw upon your courage to spread my own wings and try."

Momma deer and her babe, then out of the weeds, too, speaking much in her silent stance of what I am to do. "With grace, with gentle determination, be you as you are. Continue to keep open your compassionate heart. Our quiet way we know when to appear and when to be a shadow listening. Leverage us to help you move through life elegantly. A time to listen and a time to speak. Patience and flexibility. We will help you walk each step with poise and ease. And you as mom to

321

your dear Roo and her little sis; yes, you and I both honored to receive two special gifts."

All poised and waiting to coo, "You are loved," at least fifteen of you, my mourning doves. Your blessings as you fly over me: "Keep going, continue to embrace peace."

Two weeks and counting Australia awaits, and in six weeks our fifty-mile race. In between an anniversary of a very special day, when you unconditionally handed me faith as you stepped further away. You had always hoped I would learn surrendering; you knew trust at deeper levels my capability. I am learning not to draw a box next to each goal, no longer the need to check as complete through my control. Now on vision boards my wants and dreams, trusting—and believing I deserve—what I hope will come to be. They are singing as I run, they are standing along the path I go, sandhill cranes messaging, "You have time, take it slow."

Ensuring I call it a day, my guardian again when time to put on the brakes. Your little sis communicating "now turn off the light, time for sleep tonight." You asked her to visit at our familiar hour, at 4:00 a.m. her soft song to wake me: "Mom, I love you, and my big sis wants to speak."

"Mom, we are putting the finishing touches on one of our plans; soon it will be time for you to put the compiling of our story into another's hands. To make it matter that Earth I had to leave, to help give hope to others who may need reminders to believe. We knew our hearts would always be intertwined, part of our purpose to show others it is never good-bye. Gifts always come out of pain if we choose to see—in sorrow and grief also beauty. Mom, I am proud of you and the brave way you grew. Always our love, to the moon.

"I see Daddy and Ginger under the maple tree, a part of

the lawn you and I would sit lazily. I know our Robin isn't near, but I can't help thinking her message lingers. "New beginnings," she assured during our last days, an anchor as our hearts prepared to break. Sheltering her babes in the rain, unconditionally bearing the brunt of the wind that stormy day. Like your unconditional love of me, trying to bear my pain as you struggled to breathe. The rhythm of your heartbeat steady physically, the lurch of your heart at the thought of no longer holding me.

"You, Daddy, and Ginger are starting a new journey, a special bond as family. You are making it matter, Mom. You are honoring me. Thank you for the most incredible love I could ever receive. Always, Mom, always, intertwined we will be."

My beautiful Roo, you brought me to me.

I promise to do all I can to give purpose to the gift of you I received. You live on through me every step I take; you may be a little further but you are not far away. The essence of me is the essence of you. To the moon and back, my beautiful Roo.

UNCONDITIONALLY

August 15, 2015

Part 2

Dear Roo, when I too reach my last hours may life's reflection show me: I lived to the fullest who you helped me to be.

My wants, hopes, dreams.

Like the ebb and flow of a river that rages, slows, rises, falls, straightens, and bends, but never doesn't flow. She and her dear husband celebrating seventy years of marriage, forever joined souls. Told once that their light could not be told apart, they blend together two beats joined as one heart. That they connect between lifetimes, how much their souls fueled by the other to love, grow, and play. An essence of her the unconditional love he has always gave.

Always a dog by her side, her guardian on Earth through the chapters of her life. Her eyes looked into the eyes of a soul in a fur coat; she knew who looked back was more powerful than gold. Surrounded by Universal love, she was humbled and awed, a best friend spelled backward—DOG equals GOD. She didn't have children of her own for she had a purpose to serve many more. She did not need two legs to still know the definition of what "mother" stood for.

Nature her meditation, Nature her centering, Nature her teacher, Nature her BE-ing. She ran, hiked, bicycled, kayaked, and walked too, all over the world, all seven continents, until her last breath was through. Races and longer endurance events part of her every year her second half of life; those kind of events her closest to complete mind, body, spirit she would find. Her sister her coconspirator in experiencing the world, annual sis trips, birthday mystery plans, lunch dates not far away. Whatever they did, was not as important as "getting it," as knowing that in each other's hearts was reserved a large space.

She was of service on boards, in writing, in a listening ear, she reminded others in their doubt, "The other side so very near." Her soul soared at learning and at being a beacon of hope, trust, and faith; calmness and only seeing "can," no matter the struggle faced. Her passion to create insatiable, her quest to learn, stretch, and grow; newness she craved, courageously exploring she would go.

Her foundation to see purpose taking place in all things, her words weaving hope like an elegant tapestry. Her writing was a blend of beauty, just as her life well lived, giving to others in cocreation with the Universe her wonderful and amazing gift.

To complete the puzzle pieces of others' lives, while she connected all the pieces of hers, the wings she outstretched to see, travel, and experience places all over the world. Hard to leave her family, hard not to go, her peace that she always came back a better person for her loves at home.

"Nothing is coincidence, everything happens exactly as it should" guided her every moment of every day. It continued to open her heart wider and wider, incredible trust, bravery, and faith.

She cocreated books to teach the world love, faith, and hope; her written obituaries, eulogies, and tributes capturing the essence of a passed from this life soul. She began working from home full-time (her Earth guardian[s] so filled with joy), her log cabin often her desk for all she would write. Her cause was to heal hearts, to help beauty be seen in pain, to inspire others to see through loss there is always gain. Her ability to see and hear helped many not lose their ability to see, the power of unconditional love also what she strived to help others believe. She called them her whispers, her cocreators of hope, faith, and love, a direct link to be messenger for those above.

"Four hundred and seventy-two people to her scrapbook, twentyfold," moments, seasons, lifetimes, each one a puzzle piece guiding her to old. Her lifetime unfolded her into a beautiful soul, her faith taught us how we never walk alone. She was compassionate, yet determined, she was somewhat bold, yet she was grace, she knew when to walk elegantly under the TV, she knew when to step onto center stage. Her life well lived indeed, she and Pete an amazing "we," thousands

Upon thousands of lives touched for the better

Through the essence of me.

August 22, 2015

Peace and tranquility, as we paddled in rhythm, symbolism of our mantra in life, "Flow downstream." Tradition started by my sister, now for each annually; birthday celebrations months after the day, planned mysteries. A gift with a message, "Pick a date then you shall see"; surprises unfold through love abundantly.

The herons on our path reinforce our certain knowing; with the current of life we are flowing. And you as guardian gracing my planned day. Your wings gently gliding across the waterway. Beautiful Hawk in silent majesty, your assurance always with me.

Rituals and traditions, routines and fond memories. The foundation to build upon with new beginnings. Like anchors for my soul, as it grows and unfolds, sureness, safeness, heart's home. The base gently, firmly, solidly whispers, "Stretch your wings"—the platform that promises not to falter, my grounding, to ever trust and believe.

Sis trips that include a slumber party, pizza, and a sweet treat too; laughter to tears and a deepening friendship through each adventure we do. Each other's sounding board, each other's base, and each other's encouragement to forego fears, to be brave. Kayaking new, dinner at a favorite place, our pajama party in a different way. Under the stars, by the light of a special moon; a tent, a bonfire, s'mores, sisterhood as a beacon shining through.

Another tradition I have not been able to revisit on my own for many a year.

This year excitement to bring the memory near.

German chocolate cake with coconut-pecan frosting. A la mode with more nuts in the form of butter pecan ice cream. His favorite on his birthdays, part of our meal this year to celebrate. He would have been sixty-eight this year had he felt on Earth he could stay. This time I was ready to fully honor him, no longer harboring pain. My Roo, through your support to release the "unworthy," to forgive, and love, the past of me. Unconditional love now given, coursing through easily. "Dad, my heart in gratitude. In honor of, and to give purpose as you would want your Kit to do. Happy birthday, and thank you."

August 23, 2015

I felt your guiding love when across our path you flew; I didn't yet know the surprise you had orchestrated to occur soon. On another family trip, your daddy and Ginger escorting me, cheerleaders for my upcoming race at the start and when finishing. Taking our time on the drive to our overnight stay; back-road scenery, skipping stones on a beach walk, the setting sun winding down the day.

Awaiting the start of a race I once hadn't planned to repeat; "old" habits to not run a race twice, preferring a course of mystery. At least that was what I thought before you showed me. There is power in a circle coming back around for healing. With little sleep but an extremely determined soul, the only choice was "do this" two years ago. You weren't a guardian above to send angels my way, yet I know it was your heart still guiding that day. The door was opening further as you were teaching me; I was entering a room filled with bravery as myself to be.

At the beginning of that race, two Earth angels I received, invited to join them through each mile of all thirteen. Their spirits kept lightheartedness through the ups of each hill; only seeing *can*, certainty in *will*. That sleep was nearly absent as fuel for the day, not hindered because of their motivation every step of the way. They didn't know my heart—well, given that nothing is coincidence, perhaps they did. How very much for the sake of myself I needed this.

Now I stand at the start two years later, your daddy and Ginger to cheer me on my way. And next to me in similar wait the same two Earth angels ready to take our starting place. Recognition each of the other between the surprise and joy that swells, a brief, "Has life been treating you well?" The question shared by us three and our awe at how life's moments don't ever occur coincidentally. The familiar motivation as if two years was just yesterday; my two Earth angels to run with again this race. Every step of thirteen the power of three: inspiration, laughter, happiness—these angels and me.

Slowly, gently, I feel a widening. Are you sure, my beautiful Roo, I am ready? I was able to talk about our upcoming fifty-mile goal without pause to my heart's rhythm, without tears to inward hold. I can feel a release as you bring me additional hands to hold. Your little sis with her smile when crossing the finish line; two strangers brought back to my path, after myself I've been able to find. You are surrounding me with messengers, with guardians, with love that has always been next to me. Now, thanks to you, I recognize, I embrace,

I see.

The path of the trail the same, yet the view so differently. My soul not lost, peace and trust not fleeting. "Is that a hoot?" my running mate for the day did say. Not certain, but would not be surprised if you sent Owl to join the race. I can still feel the power of its wings over you and me that July day, its promise to bring wisdom if I was willing to let go of the reins. In four more days I leave home; another new experience, another part of the globe. My heart will feel the tug of separation, but differently; not away two nights during your final days but for two weeks your little sis I'll temporarily leave. I will begin my travels home on the day home paused being that for me; home no longer broken, but now so beautifully complete. A reflection of what I feel in my heart, a mirror of me.

September 12, 2015

I am home. I am continents away.

My heart yearns for your little sis I will see in two more days. My heart remembers one year ago today.

We made it, baby girl, as you promised when you whispered, "It is time I be on my way." My angel above, guiding my every step I take.

My morning run as the sun rose to shine its radiant beams. The dolphins with their message of play and healing. The girl who sat in front of my seat, her shoulder your wink. "Hi Mom. Always to the moon and back, our love. You and me." The tattooed crescent moon in the light of day, never, my Roo, will you be far away. The song you led me to, the lyrics "I will always remember you." The feather on my path as I walked toward a "reach for the sky" view. Abundant your messages today: "peace, no space, nor time, always with me you are by my side."

I can't find the pain anymore when I speak your name; the words no longer caught in my throat when "Roo," I say. Just as I had described you as my child in a fur coat to any stranger's inquiry, "How many children do you have?" your little sis now the one who is center stage when asked. I can gently talk about losing "our second born" as I sometimes describe you. "To cancer," I can now voice aloud without tears ready to splash from a heart's wound. My eyes light up from my soul's joy— Ginger in our lives—gratitude that she rescued your daddy's and mine.

I am experiencing today. I am reliving the hours before and after you went physically away.

Though I had already traveled through what I thought was the lowest point I would know, that familiar feeling of curling up tight was ready to take hold. The first days without you near, I slept on the floor next to your dog bed; I couldn't sleep in the "big bed" where many a night we had curled up head to head. Any space elsewhere felt too far away, as I tried to hold tightly to the trust you had gave. I could inhale the scent of you as I struggled to gain my foothold, as I prepared to grow further in faith and let go. You continued to show me we had not said, "Good-bye," that between us was no space, always by my side.

Under the star-filled night in the woods with your aunt a few weeks ago, you nudged me awake with a song's echo. The song "Stairway to Heaven" played through my mind, a reflection of the completeness I was feeling inside. True to your messages you have brought to my every day, that you have taught me each one as miracle moments individually in their own way. You have continued to reinforce my soul's growth to the center of me, stairs onto my path on this trip near our one-year anniversary.

My inner me whispering, "Is this really happening?" When my eyes beholding Australia—such awe-filled beauty. A climb to the top of a bridge as the sun awoke to the day, and you as the moon guiding the first steps made. At the Three Sisters in the Blue Mountains my soul dancing in glee, conquering one thousand steps with the exhilaration of a workout, with a graceful ease. In Honolulu, another steep climb to a view high above, my body and spirit in gratitude and love. As you taught me the parallel of running to life, so to the symbolism of a steep and upward climb. The most amazing scenery awaits us at the top, if we have the courage to believe, to not stop.

In an effort to give to you the unconditional love you gave me, I trusted and took that very large leap. You had never let me down, you promised me it would be okay. You trusted me in turn to give meaning to that day. Somehow, I think I am still more the receiver than the giver of such an incredible love. My dear Roo, my baby girl, my angel now above. The view is incredible, this sight you have given me. A trust in all moments of life, even in the painful is such beauty.

To the moon and back, my dear Roo,

Always, my love for

you.

Postscript

September 27, 2015

Mile twenty-four calling, urging, beckoning to me. "The most exciting will soon begin," I exclaim to your daddy. About to begin the second lap in familiar territory, but what I would feel as the miles increased I could not foresee. I knew I would have moments that would test my strength and would require I dig deep inside of me. I also knew the finish line I would reach.

Miles after twenty-four calling to me, "It is time to experience new things." Smaller increments of goals to achieve, marker twenty-eight, thirty-four, forty. "You have time"—so many reminders this past year that time is relative and of longevity. Leverage the downhills and smile through the climbs, keep going forward no matter the miles-per-minute time. The stillness of Nature that I would better *hear*, heartbeats of promise, no room for doubts or fears.

Never a wall of bricks brandishing a shield of "are you sure you don't want to slow down or stop and call it a day?" The most certain feeling of "I will" imprinting each footstep made. Having fun through it all the mantra I carried with me. Gratitude for my health, for the weather, for the forest beauty. Gratitude for the moon at mile forty-nine; to the moon and back my love to you, dear Roo, the finish line in sight.

A year ago we ran this race, twenty-six miles the goal celebrating your birthday. It was a first, a marathon via trail and not road; it was a first, fourteen days without you on Earth since your time to go. Not as surefooted I could travel the year ahead without you, but my promise of trust and making it matter my determination to do. Now I run eager for the miles we have not yet known, certain—oh so very certain—I will not be alone.

Mile marker forty-six, seven, eight, nine; in the distance three amazing sights. Your daddy, your little sis, and the moon's radiant light. My legs run, Ginger sings, and now she is the push behind me. Just as you are the pull in the sky: "Mom, to the moon and back. Always with you I will be. And Mom, it is time you and I both know, all things new, let go of the old."

Mile twenty-four the turning point, the intersection of my life. To the new I eagerly begin, to the old I say thank you and good-bye. The first half the foundation that has made me
Me.

The second half in trust of who I choose to be, belief in every mile I cannot yet see. Across the finish, joy coursing through me. Last year, tears of grief. This year, open arms to all life holds—it's uphill and downhill incredible breathtaking, and breath giving, beauty to see.

It is the day after we achieved fifty miles, the day of your actual birthday. In the dark I sit, a wink from you I await. As the eclipse begins, your promise stays strong. Always by my side, and even when dark, light is never gone. As the red of the eclipse blankets the moon, the stars more brilliant to view. With peace wrapped around my heart like the blanket of red covering you, in the near distance, your message through the serenade: "hoot hoot."

"Mom, thank you for giving back to me, the most precious love yours unconditionally. Through trusting as you did when you walked with me my last days, in letting go you were so very brave. You continued to watch, to look, to see. You gained certainty, a stronger foundation in the ability to believe. Now you are ready to walk your life trail with my little sis; she has much to teach you about hearing, among her purpose and her gifts. Your love of words to communicate will continue to gain their strength, as you learn to listen without words in each step you take. 'The art of hearing heartbeats,' a mantra you embrace. Close your eyes, listen. Ah, yes, the steady beat through space."

"Happy birthday, dear Roo. These stars, with Owl, in love and in peace—to the moon and back, I love you. Oh my! As if you need to reinforce the power of these two days, a shooting star you have just sent my way. I wish I may, I wish I might. From this day forward, I embrace all new to life."

I will always make it matter, Roo, the life you lived and gave that I might fully live. Thank you for leading me to the center of myself, my beautiful—so beautiful—gift.

Acknowledgments

When you are someone who believes there is a reason why every person crosses our path, it is hard to narrow a list for expressing appreciation to those who contributed to *To the Moon and Back...to Me: What I Learned from Four Running Feet.*

To my lifetime Trifecta whose birthday gift led me to a writer's workshop.

Which led to the start of a mentorship with author Wade Rouse, who gave me the gift of not only his time but his expertise and his critique.

He gave me the gift of courage to share my heart as he so beautifully does on paper and in person.

And he gave me the gift of believing in my voice.

Which led to the honor of receiving professional editing for this book from Nikki Busch, who gave not only her exceptional skill but a perfect blend of respect for what was written with a keen eye to what could be better said.

She too gave me the gift of her encouragement and faith that this book was meant to be.

Which led to my third honor of working with a very talented and intuitive artist, Deborah Bradseth, who not only designed a cover that captured the essence of this memoir, she ensured the book formatting was publish-ready.

She compassionately reminded me I can do this when the reality so very near was a little overwhelming—in an exciting kind of way.

I am in gratitude to each of you for walking these last steps of this journey with me. I love words, and yet I find it hard to adequately write my heartfelt thanks.

But then again, because of your part in getting to here—I know you know my heart.

Thank you.

Lightning Source UK Ltd.
Milton Keynes UK
UKHW041243290621
386344UK00002B/701

9 780997 344929